An Invitation to Suicide

Faris Al-Timimi

Disclaimers

Fiction This is a work of fiction. Names, characters, places, and incidents either are the product of the author's imagination or are used fictitiously. Any resemblance to actual persons, living or dead, events, or locales is entirely coincidental.

Imagery Any people depicted in stock imagery provided by Thinkstock are models, and such images are being used for illustrative purposes only.

Publisher Information

Art and Novels Inc. 16 Munro Street
Thorold, Ontario, L2V 2V8
Canada

Contact: artandnovels@gmail.com

Edition History

- **First Published:** 2017
- **Second Edition:** 2026

An Invitation to Suicide

The lesson is not the events of the story!

It is the value and behavior of

those who create the events!
The best story, a story does not end and does not fade, a story,

continues with the characters and events, to live and recur!

Faris Al-Timimi

Dedication

To all those who have been disenfranchised,
To those whose wills have been robbed,
To those who are forced to obey the wills of others.

The Depressing Morning

In the morning, Bob opens the door of his home to go out, shuffling hesitantly. This is not how he would usually leave home to go to work at his company. Normally, he would come out aggressively, stepping vigorously and seriously, but today, he comes out as if strong hands are preventing him from going any further, heading toward his car which is parked on the driveway in front of the garage door. He opens the car door and sits down behind the steering wheel with an absent and shattered mind. He is hesitant for a few moments before starting the car engine, which is something he was not used to. He slows down his movements; he did not really want to go to the office, but, at the same time, he is driven by a strong desire to explore what was happening outside—outside of his home—and to learn more about the event more comprehensively.

He turns the car key to run the engine, then, a few seconds later, presses the button of the radio, trying to listen to the news—he, who did not used to listen to the news in his car. He does not even know the news frequencies on the radio; he kept changing the radio stations, trying to find one of the news channels he was familiar with. His attempts did not seem to provide him with what he was looking for. Then he felt that maybe it was better to press the radio button again to enjoy the tranquility of the drive as he set off on his way to his office.

Everything around him this morning seemed bleak; the air seemed heavy and saturated with moisture, although the sky was almost clear, and only a few white clouds were scattered here and there, suspended and swimming in a clear blue sky. Such a scene would appear to anyone else like a morning full of promise and happiness. To Bob, this morning was not like that, but he realizes that this has nothing to do with what he feels right now and the actual truth, and that the gloom he is experiencing is only limited to his internal feelings, caused both by what is going on outside in the news but also, perhaps, actual events around him, and that this is nothing more than a coincidence and has nothing to do with this exotic "call." He is not one of those who believe that nature should respond and become depressed when people decide to behave badly, or when they commit a crime against themselves or others.

He also has frequently passed over such positions, when some transient phenomena may have indicated what seemed to have something to do with a particular event occurring sometime, somewhere, but it soon turned out later that these phenomena were in reality nothing but matters of abstracted coincidences. Man only tends to pay attention to these coincidences when going through difficult times and when mentally occupied by shocking events, hence the misbelief that everything happens because of, and related to, the said event. This misbelief is also because man has always believed that he is the center of the universe and that everything that happens around him is related to him and meant for him.

Bob is always realistic and pragmatic in his way of thinking and living. Since he reached maturity, he has realized that life is not going to stop nor care because of the decision of anyone to go to the left or the right, and life would never change its direction if millions of people for any reason decided to live this life or not. At the beginning of his journey, when he was still in the inner streets of the upscale residential compound where his home is located, it seemed to him that the luxury homes today were more silent, rigid, and lifeless than normal and seemed devoid of their usual luster, elegance, and beauty. The streets of the compound were lifeless, or, at least, that's how they seemed to him, but that might have been due to his particular depression that day because of the strange, bizarre news.

When he reached the end of the compound street, he turned to the right to merge into the main street, which he used to take almost five days every week, driving to his office. He began to look right and left as he drove at a slow speed, compared to his normal speed which he went at every day on the same street. It was also not teeming with traffic and people heading to work like it was last week. The street did not look as clean as it used to be, or, maybe this was how he felt or imagined it to be.

In fact, nothing was the same as it used to be. Only a few things still looked normal. The early morning coffee and donut shops and some fast-food services seem to be open, but those who had opened did not seem to have as many customers as usual, and maybe they were not fully staffed, or, perhaps they were being run by their owners who were serving customers. Some of the gas stations had a "closed" sign! Bob did not know what life on the street had looked like for the past four days because he hadn't left home for the past four days because he'd had a cold. He had not left home since last Thursday.

Street scenes and life seem to have changed considerably, as far as Bob is concerned, or at least as he perceives them. Many people obviously did not leave their homes, or, maybe they have stayed somewhere, somehow. Some of them might have thought staying indoors was a form of solidarity with the advocates of the "call"—the invitation to collective suicide. Perhaps some of them are waiting for more specific information, more clarity, so that they can express their opinion and base their position on a better understanding. And some of them probably decided to pause for a moment of introspection to consider what is going on in their lives and to make up their minds with regard to the "call." Finally, some can't, or maybe do not dare for other reasons, respond to the "call."

But the fact is, there are many who despise this invitation and those who are behind it, simply because they enjoy a comfortable, prosperous life and have no objections to its way of functioning, and it does not cross their minds any day to give up their lives, nor to make a sacrifice of any aspect of it, while they are enjoying it to the full!

All of these expectations and perceptions were conflicting in his mind and contributed to his lack of focus on a lot of what appeared to him and what he saw on the street. He thought for a moment that it was not wise to leave home today and go out before it became clearer to him what was happening outside in this big city where he lives. But he couldn't wait any longer… He is the kind of person who used to take charge of events and explores the reality of things by himself; he never liked to sit back and wait for others to tell him what is going on or their interpretation of things. That is how he lived his life. He considered his keenness and interest in his way of living the main factors of his success in work and life.

Many old memories and perceptions went on to inspire his imagination. Many of those images were from his past, his personal life, and the life of his family—Nicola, his wife, and his son and daughter, Jonathan and Josephine, who live their own lives independently, and about his three grandchildren, and the luxurious life available to him and his family compared with the lives experienced by others. This might explain why people reject their lives and call for this collective suicide. He recalled his younger years when he began his business operations, struggling to achieve economic and social status above the level of what he was living, and that the success he achieved was far more than what he dreamed of and expected.

Yes, he was a fighter, struggling and patient, but he was also fully aware that what he had achieved and reached in business success was not only due to his own capabilities, and that most of it was achieved by the creativity and effort of those who worked with him from the beginning, and then later worked under him and served him, including many who until now were still working for him in his company. But their lives have never changed nor improved from what they were years ago. He is fully aware that life does not always reward everyone who works hard and may even crush a lot of those hard-working, creative people. He is certainly aware and believes that a lot of luck and opportunity are also involved in success.

It is clear that this is not an invitation advocated by a religious group, or, at least this is what Bob believes, as it does not seem to be based on religious principles or motives promoted and planned by the same previous religious cults and clans throughout the last four or five decades, which ended in just their believers' suicide. It is not, apparently, a "call" based on faith or ideology. This is very unlikely, since it is well known that believers and advocates of ideologies would never think of abandoning their permanent quest to earn as much as possible of life's privileges, even if it has prolonged its deprivation of them, no matter how seriously they claim that they do not pay attention to the benefits for themselves. This is not what they believe in, and not what they work for in their lives.

So, who could be those who are calling for this public invitation, which is probably believed to be the strangest "call" perhaps in the history of mankind? These many memories, concerns, misgivings, and perceptions went on circling in his head while he was still driving slowly, trying to identify the variables in the street on his way to his office, and these questions continued to spin in his head.

Are they the Communists? Or, maybe they are those who consider themselves Socialists? Or the Leftists, who are indirectly calling for this? There have been a lot of hidden, mysterious, obscure intentions and plans that accompanied calls for communism and maybe even socialism. Could this possibly be one of them? Or is it a capitalist plan? Capitalists always manage to get by in difficult crises. Is it those who often create crises in order to afterward rebound with more financial interest and benefits, such as happens repeatedly with stock exchange crashes and recoveries when they go to higher levels again, without anyone really knowing a convincing justification for the decline or for the rise?

All this and much more took place and continued going on in his mind to the extent he was about to hit a running dog! He was not used to seeing pets running astray, such as this loose dog running in the streets of this high-end side of the city, where he has been living for several years and where mostly only rich people live.

Finally, Bob reached the building where his office was located, and he headed toward the basement gate, toward the car park entrance, and soon a new thought entered his mind: "What if the gate did not respond to the remote key? What would happen then?" But this worry quickly dissipated when the door responded and opened up as usual. He felt a sigh of relief and brightened up when he saw it still working as usual, and then he thought that this fear was excessive and unjustified.

Then he drove inside the basement car park until he reached his parking spot. Then he switched off the car's engine and remained sitting for a few minutes contemplating and looking forward through the windshield while sitting inside the car in the parking lot, without there being anything actually significant to be seen. He was a bit reluctant to proceed to the next step, which was heading to the office. He looked like his mind was shattered, as if he was trying to focus on what was going to happen next. What was going to happen after he got out of his car?

He noticed the car park was not full today. In fact, there were still many empty spots, which was rare at this time in the morning on a Monday. He wondered where the car owners had gone who usually used these now-vacant parking spots. Although it was almost certain that it was related to this strange call, that was not his main concern now. He needed to go to the elevator. He was keen, yet apprehensive at the same time. He wanted to see who had come to the office as usual and who hadn't. He was worried at the same time about whether the elevator would work as usual. If the elevator did not work, he would have to go up the stairs to the fifty-sixth floor of the building, where his office is located, and he didn't think he could do that.

Bob thought to himself, "My God, we never think about how much time and effort is needed to maintain all the things we live with and use. How many people are there in the background whom we take for granted."

He arrived with his slow, reluctant, unusual steps at the six gates of the elevators. The first thing he looked at was the elevator lights, which were illuminated as usual and which, therefore, meant that the elevators were supposed to be working as usual, or so he hoped. He pressed the elevator button, and one of the doors opened quickly, as if the elevator was waiting for him and no one had used it for at least a few minutes. He entered the elevator and then pressed the number '56' button and the door closed. Then the lift started to move up all the way without stopping at any of the floors on the way. Bob followed the movement of the elevator at its usual speed and hoped that it wouldn't suddenly stop for any reason.

It did not take long before the lift reached the fifty-sixth floor, and then the door opened. Bob walked out of it into the corridor in front of the elevator doors and then walked along the corridor leading to his office. He did not meet any of the staff of the other companies which share this floor and also did not see any visitors. Normally he would see many visitors, but it was very quiet today, far more than usual, or that's how it seemed to him. He did not care much for the quietness in the long corridor, and he wished his steps would reach his office quickly. He reached it, opened the door, and went straight to his office, passing by the group of small open-plan offices separated by glass barriers. He turned his head toward these offices to see who was there. He only saw two staff members out of more than the ten employees who normally work for him at the head office. He greeted them remotely as he used to, saying:

"Good morning."

Both returned the greeting. He noticed his secretary, who used to wait for him, was not there this morning. His concerns increased, but he did not show anything when he greeted two of the staff who were sitting in their small offices. He didn't see the cleaners who would normally be cleaning the offices at this time of day. This morning, he saw no one— could this only be another coincidence?

He entered his room, took his jacket off, threw it on one of the chairs, and went to sit at the desk chair. He sat down, trying to relax; he leaned on the desk, supporting his arms on it, intertwining his fingers and looking toward the door. His mind is obviously far away from his position in the office. He could not focus his mind on any particular thing... He did not feel the desire to switch on the computer, nor the TV; he was only trying to calm down the indescribable feelings and obsessive thoughts which he had not experienced before. It seemed like a big problem, or that is what he thought. Maybe other people thought the same, but he has not yet found out or guessed what a serious impact it could have on society. What kind of effect could it inflict on him and his company and the future of his family? To what extent could it be real, and how long would it last? Is it a local "call," or does it cover the entire country? Or, maybe, it really is an international "call" as some news agencies suggest?

He turned to the back while sitting at his desk to face the wide window and look out through it to the distant horizon, which is obscured by the many high-rise buildings. He felt that, in spite of their grandeur and prestige, there was no sign of life or activity in them. In fact, the whole scene did not look normal. It looked frozen, devoid of any movement at all. Maybe because it was not easy to identify things from this towering height, he couldn't easily see the details of the people from this altitude, perhaps because he did not pay attention to details, or he was not concerned about this when he was previously looking from his elevated position.

How could a person decide to sacrifice and give up his life, to end it by himself willingly? It is really a difficult thing to imagine. But isn't this what we know as suicide? Isn't this the same thing we have heard of since time immemorial? We know that it was probably a sacred act for some people and tribes in the past, when people who had been defeated chose to do it of their own free will. Indeed, they saw it as a matter of honor. But what has happened to make such a "call" appear in this day and age? Our modern world is remote from such ideals of honor and dignity, which were held in such high regard. Indeed, such values only face mockery and contempt from most people.

Suddenly, there was a knock at the door, and it opened straight away. A confused but serious-looking middle-aged woman quickly apologized for being late. It was Christine, his secretary and office manager. Bob quickly responded and stood up as if he was eagerly waiting for her arrival. He told her not to bother about being late and seemed to be relieved that she had come to work. He asked her to take a seat and he walked around from behind the desk to come closer to her, wondering and waiting eagerly to hear her answer—any answer—to his question:

"What is happening?"

He had been pondering this question for some time, and he was waiting for the right moment to approach her with it. It also seemed that he wanted to hear the answer—any answer—from her. But she responded by repeating her apology for being late and insisted on mentioning the reason for her delay in detail, saying that she had to take her son and daughter to school by herself because the school bus had not turned up and that, when she had arrived at the school, she had only found a few parents who were standing outside the school building waiting with their children, trying to find out any news about the situation, whether the school would open or not, and whether the teachers would come in or not.

But it seems that nothing was guaranteed in her opinion, so she preferred not to wait too long and decided to take her children to her mother's house at the other end of the big city, and this was briefly the reason for the delay. But it was clear that the confusion was not only because of these delays, but, apparently, was much more than that. It was evident from her talk, her confusion, and the reluctance and hesitation when she described what had happened that she was really frightened and that there were other things on her mind, more important and probably dangerous. Bob asked her why she looked troubled and confused, but she assured him that nothing was wrong. However, he was sure that she was upset, and he kept on encouraging her to focus her attention and respond to his questions. So, he asked again:

"What is going on outside? I mean in the city?"

He was talking about the "call" for collective suicide and who could be advocating it. He thought he might be able to find out something from her about those people who believe in it and expect it to be carried out. Are there real people who are prepared for its implementation? It was important for him to know how much she knew about this call for suicide. This is because he sees her as important in his daily life, as she belongs to the middle class and, perhaps, also the poor class. She, as a person, had a serious and committed personality. She had worked hard as his office manager for almost eight years, and he knows that she is very ambitious for her husband and children. She puts up with inconveniences and difficulties in her daily life because of her family's economic situation and their limited financial resources.

Many other unanswered thoughts revolved in his head, some relatively simple, such as:

"You know I don't care about or believe what is published in the newspapers and other media, which is why I don't remember many details about the basis of the 'call' and how seriously it should be taken. You know that the week does not end without reading many sensational headlines in the papers, TV, the Internet, political statements, corporate news, and the stock markets, and I don't pay it much attention or even believe in one percent of it. If I believed everything that was said, I don't think I could've built this small empire." As he said it, he pointed to his office and the other small offices which comprised his company.

Christine replied:

"Yes, yes, I know that..." but she soon started stuttering again. She was bewildered and couldn't really carry on talking.

He held her, trying to help her focus. It was the first time he had held her, but he felt that he had to because she was on the verge of collapse. She, in turn, did not care and was not surprised that he was holding her, but she asked him to let her sit down to recover. He took her to one of the chairs and asked her if she would like to drink something. He seemed confident that her unusual state was because of the "call," so he insisted on following her up and giving her his full attention to see what she would say. At the same time, she hesitated and felt ashamed to ask her employer for something, but it is clear that she was suffering terribly mentally, and that made it easy for her to ask him for a cup of water because she would not normally have been so presumptuous. Bob rushed to the refrigerator in his office, bringing her a small bottle of water. He opened it and gave it to her. She thanked him, took it, and rushed to drink it with a quick and confused sip, and then, when she had finished, she went to look in the direction of the big, broad office window while still holding the water bottle.

She muttered quietly, "I can't believe it..."

He surprisingly noticed what she said and anxiously responded, "What is it that you can't believe?"

She repeated her words again, "I cannot believe he means what he says, and that he can do it!"

She spoke while still gazing into the distance, her face growing paler, and her eyes terrified. It was as if she was looking at a fixed target, while, in fact, there was no target. Bob went on and repeated his question to her, "What is it that you cannot believe? Who are you talking about?"

"John ... John, my husband."

She stammered again the words of her reply and turned her head towards Bob and was about to burst into tears. Then she went once again to look through the wide window and appeared terrified as if she had lost her mind. She was clearly terrified of something serious!

"What is it John wants to do?" He asked her in a surprised tone.

She replied, "…he wants to go with those people!"

"What people?" He responded a bit sharper and tougher this time, as if he had discovered an important thread in his attempt to solve the mystery about this cult of people who are following the "call." Then he grabbed her again and shook her, as she sat on the chair, in order to get her to pay attention and focus. He was still keenly awaiting her answers and was expecting her to speak up clearly and promptly, just like she did in her job.

Bob is always like this, a practical man who believes that time should not be wasted stuttering and mumbling, especially when the subject is already ambiguous. He was desperate to find out as much as possible about it.

Then she recovered and said, "He, I mean John, believes he should support this call, and he says there is no point of living and no benefit we can expect from this life … Can you believe this?"

Bob was shocked to hear this and, terrified, he replied, "Can I believe what? Which call does John want to follow? What life are you talking about? What exactly are you saying? Do you mean he wants to go with those people the media are talking about, those who do not want to live any more, the ones who are preparing for suicide, like those stupid and ridiculous ones who lost their minds and committed suicide. The ones who killed themselves with explosives in order to kill other innocent people, believing they are sending a sacred message, a message of delusion, a message of faith, that they will soon go to another world, a better world, a world of delusion and faith, a world which does not exist, apart from in their own imaginations and delusions!"

Bob continued in his passionate narrative as if he was actively arguing or debating with one of those people, the ones who are preparing to commit suicide for ideological reasons. Christine herself returned to her confused state again looking at and through the wide windows, while he continued to complete his words about what he thinks of those people, trying to reassure her that it is just the sick imagination and misconception of those people, and that it cannot be transformed into reality, and he really does not know how or why she believes it.

But he suddenly realized that he had not given her the chance to talk, as much as he had talked himself about those deluded people and their "call," and noticed that she had become agitated again, which told him that she had not really listened to his criticisms of those who were calling for suicide. He had not given her the opportunity to continue and finish her answer, so, he returned to her in order to get her attention back and realized that he didn't know much about John, because he had never bothered to ask her about him before. He remembered that he had met him only briefly on one or two transients, when the company was inviting the employees and other guests to small receptions to celebrate successful deals or commercial business achievements. It could be that John is a religious person who believes in such superstitions. Or maybe he is someone who is suffering from an illness or psychological condition. A lot of people have clearly been affected like this in recent years.

It might also be that Christine herself exaggerated the situation in her own mind and so her reaction was also exaggerated. It could also be the result of a personal problem between Christine and her husband. Any of this could be true. However, this time, he thought back to what he had heard about the "call" from what he saw yesterday when he was watching the TV news about the people who were calling for collective suicide, and how some TV channels had alerted viewers that they might be short staffed because a lot of the young staff members and technical workers have announced that they intend to participate in the "call" either as observers or perhaps actually committing suicide! However, some will just follow the news and maybe meet the people who are actively involved in it.

He also remembered what he heard last night from a press report, that this audacious "call" is open to anyone who wants to accept, adopt and implement it. It would be left up to each individual person to choose the time and method of execution, and this is what made him and his wife Nicola stay up late last night before they went to bed. But they had barely managed to sleep because of the horror of what was going to happen and how far spread it might be. My God, how could he misunderstand it?

Images started to pass before his eyes, reminding him of how it was when he woke up in the morning, how difficult it was to get up from his bed when he hadn't slept well and how he had found that his wife, Nicola, had woken up first. When he came down to the ground floor, he found her standing in the kitchen leaning on the kitchen counter, looking as if she was deep in thought. She was absentmindedly holding her coffee mug in her hand, when he greeted her and asked if she had had enough sleep. She didn't really answer his question, but responded by asking him, or maybe asking herself, "Could something like this really happen? Is it possible we could see another Oklahoma, or a new 911 and of our own free will this time? And this time, will it be announced in advance on the TV and in the papers? Where are we going?"

"It seems that we are going to see something new this time. The last few years have been eventful, and they are still impacting on us. But now we must consider the unthinkable. All the same, we must now hope that this is just a nightmare!"

Yes, it is really serious, and he knows it and is convinced of it. So how come he goes back trying to appear normal before his secretary, Christine. He put on his usual managerial persona of knowing more than she knows.

He knows what a serious time it is, and believes that it will carry on being even more unimaginable now and it is very likely that Christine knows more than he knows, but maybe the information she has through her husband is what he needs and would like to know now, so, again, he turned to her, pulled the chair to come closer to her and try to comfort her to find out what she knows about this thing, particularly through her husband, as he is not only a listener to this call, like most others, but he is supporting it. That means he must know a lot more about it!

He grabbed her gently this time, after he sat on the chair, and tried to regain his composure, repeating his question. But he couldn't hide his keenness and desire to get an answer, "What does John say? Did you say he wants… or do you think he was thinking of responding to the call, I mean the invitation of those people?"

He pointed his hand subconsciously outwards towards his office door, and she quickly responded to his pointing, and soon turned her head toward the door as if she had been terrified and alarmed of something. She whispered a soft scared voice, wondering, "Whom do you mean by those people? Do we have any of them here in the company?"

He quickly replied, "No, no, no. I didn't mean a particular person here. I don't know any of them. But it's possible that we might have one or maybe more than one. I don't know now. Didn't you notice that a lot of our employees didn't show up today as usual?"

Then she said, "No, I didn't pay any attention when I entered the office. I just wanted to come and see you and explain why I was late. I didn't notice whether people were in their offices or not, I mean our staff." She stopped for a moment and before he could interrupt her, she went on, "Everyone of them could have had his own reasons, as I had my reasons for being late. I'll go out now and see who is in."

He grabbed her shoulder to keep her sitting there, saying, "Don't, it doesn't matter now, leave it for later."

She interrupted him saying, "It will only take a minute, and I can see if anyone who did not come in has left a message on the answering machine."

He wanted to keep her there by saying again, "Don't, just leave this matter now, let's go back to what you were saying about John."

Then he was silent for a moment, and looked into her eyes, as if he was certain for the first time that he knew someone who believed in the "call" and then went on to finish by asking, "Do you really think John means what he says?"

She rushed to interrupt him even though she was distracted and unable to control her movements, "He means what?"

Bob replied, "I mean, do you think he means what he says about his belief in the summons of those people who want to end their lives?" This time he avoided pointing towards the door.

She responded quickly and confidently, "Yes, yes, I think he meant what he said to me." Then she added, "I know John means what he told me, and, I know he has his own reasons!"

Bob disapprovingly interrupted her, "His own reasons? What do you mean by 'he has his own reasons'? What reasons could he have to make him prefer death to life? I mean suicide! How could he leave you and your two beautiful children? I've seen their pictures on your desk!"

Christine suddenly and unexpectedly broke down in tears. Bob did not know what to do to calm her and cheer her up in order to get her to continue talking to him, particularly now that they were both getting to the heart of the matter.

He tried to comfort her in any way he could, but it was clear that she was crying because of profound, very sensitive reasons. Seconds later she stuttered while she was staring at his face in a way he could not comprehend or explain, "What have they done wrong? They are innocent children. They don't understand or know good from evil. How can this be fair?"

Bob interrupted her quickly, "What children? ... Do you mean..." He tried to remember her children's names struggling, and, eventually, after a few seconds delay he came up with two names which seemed closest to their names. Then he asked a second time, "Do you mean Sarah and Danny?"

She quickly replied, correcting the names, "Suzanne and Tommy, my only two children."

She knew he did not know their right names.

"Yes, yes, of course, I'm confused, I'm sorry. What about your children? What is it to do with them? What have they got to do with all this chaos going on?"

He finished, waiting for her answer, but she was still distracted, holding her head in her hands, staring at the floor, as if she had just received terrible news. He asked her the same thing again, saying her name twice "Christine, Christine" to get her to take notice.

She responded to his entreaties and turned her head towards him, silently trying to focus her eyes on his face. He noticed a strange look on her face which he did not really understand. However, he calmed down inside, as he thought she was focused on him, so she would probably be able to give more specific answers. She took a few moments in her abstracted silence before she answered. But her answer was a terrible shock.

"John believes it would be better for me and the kids to accept this call like him!!"

She started shedding tears again but tried to not to emotionally collapse in front of him. But she couldn't control herself, and he could do nothing this time. What she had said had stunned and overwhelmed him to such an extent that he couldn't respond to her. He was speechless and didn't know what to say to her at first. Is it possible that she is serious or could she be temporarily insane? So, he asked her if she really agrees with what John had said to her. Before that he also needs to know if she is convinced that John will carry out his threat and if she believes in what he intends to do or not. However, he has definitely found out from their conversation the fact that, basically, John really believes in this alien, bold "call" to end life. Otherwise, he would not have invited his wife with their two children to join him on his ill planned trip into the unknown. All these questions passed at lightning speed through his mind, just like when thoughts flash through our minds in life threatening moments, such as when facing death, or you think you are about to face death. He had experienced that feeling of helplessness more than once, like the time when he was about to drown in a swimming pool, or when he had a horrific traffic accident when he had fallen asleep while he was driving and the car had turned over and crashed. He couldn't stop himself from following this terrifying train of thought and was distracted for several moments, until Christine herself broke into his reverie by asking him a question which reached his ears like an echo coming from a far distant place, "Do you think he is right in what he thinks?"

This time she was the one who was asking a question, and he was the one who had got lost in his thoughts. Her question took him by surprise as if it had been aimed at and asked of thousands of successful people like him. People to whom life had been kind and always smiled upon and had given them everything they ever wanted. Her question was still knocking on the doors of every one of those successful people expecting a response. Then he turned to her after a while and responded with a question of his own, "Whom do you mean? What do you mean by 'is he right'? What is right and in what respect? Don't tell me you are asking if John's behavior is right when he is thinking of ending his life? You certainly realize that someone like me cannot support this ridiculous, absurd idea of suicide. I cannot endorse or justify any suicidal ideas, whatever the motives and circumstances!"

She interrupted him by asking, "Even if the alternative is an eternal life of servitude to others?"

Quickly and firmly, Bob replied, "Yes, yes, yes!"

But he soon took account of what she has just said, and he turned towards her, bearing in mind her words of explanation, "Even if the alternative was an eternal life of servitude to others?"

He sharply repeated her words and said, "Even if the alternative was an eternal life of servitude to others? What do you mean by that?"

He hesitated and then went on saying, "I think we are now talking about a serious subject, and we really have to talk calmly and clearly. I think it's important to know each other more and to understand what we are talking about. I can't hide that our conversation has confused me."

She tried to interrupt him by apologizing, but he stopped her more firmly this time by saying, "No, you don't need to apologize, an apology cannot help here, as it won't change anything. You are not mistaken. You didn't say anything wrong to me, so you don't have to apologize."

She apologized to him again, but out of politeness and in a more friendly tone, while he continued, saying, "I think we need to reappraise ourselves from time to time about many things, especially those that we take for granted. I definitely think we should do that and now I think it's better to say that I believe in this. We take for granted that parents are devoted to their children but today I have heard about a father who is trying to convince his wife to take their two children into the unknown. What kind of unknown? An unknown which can only be attained through the ultimate sacrifice and a willingness to give up the paradox of life, a decision which cannot be changed once it has been made. I am sure that we always used to believe that it is a natural human instinct to cling to life, whatever difficulties we may face. Today, we are contradicting this basic human characteristic as we are expecting people to willingly sacrifice their lives."

"How many illusions which we once believed in do we still accept? How many parents have killed their children for imaginary, mythical, stupid reasons. Although it's possible that some of them were suffering from psychosis or depression. This has happened more than once in our society. I don't think we have done enough to stop such events. I think we're going to discover lots of things that we were dealing with every day without knowing what they are. I think one day soon we'll find out how much we insist on a lot of things. We should admit our ignorance and not forget this when we establish the rules for our lives."

He was talking as if he was frantically babbling to himself. He was aware of this and tried to speak more normally by saying, "I think we need to take the opportunity to rest and relax a bit now. Time has passed by very quickly and it is almost lunchtime. What do you think if we sneak out to have lunch in my usual restaurant and look on today as a day off. I think we have already done a lot of business in the past few weeks, and today I think we have discovered a lot of things which we did not previously know, or so it seems. So, this day off and lunch break could help us recuperate and maybe find a solution to the problem John is experiencing. Maybe we can get him to change his mind."

Although she was listening to him she did not comment and was clearly still worried. But she did not hesitate to look at him with a faded smile, when she heard that he was interested in what John was going through and hoped he might have a solution to the problem. Bob is a person with both personal and financial power who can do things which she, or any of her family members, could not do. She also felt somewhat relieved when she heard what he said about helping John and his idea of inviting her to have lunch with him at his favorite restaurant, one of the finest restaurants frequented by businessmen, especially at lunchtime, where they discuss deals. She knows very well that she would never have another opportunity to go to such a restaurant. She would not even dare to think about it. Lunch there would easily cost more than she could earn in four or five working days in her position as director of his office. Although she was overwhelmed by her worries she came back to her senses on hearing him telling her to get ready to leave for lunch. She replied, "I just need to go to my desk quickly to check what has happened. I haven't been in the office for the last three days."

He replied, "Yes, take your time, but don't be late. Anything related to work can wait. I feel tired of everything today. I don't want to check anything related to work."

She listened carefully to his words with surprise and amazement, as he had never spoken about this before today. He always used to say that work gives life a meaning. Of course he meant the intended course of his own life, and if it was not for his job, he would not have felt that his life had any meaning. He doesn't know how he will be able to live when he retires, which is a few years away, when his health is no longer burdened with work and worrying about serious things and decision making. Christine answered him positively and quickly headed towards the office door. As she reached out to open the door she remembered that she should call the restaurant to book a table for two. She turned toward Bob and asked him, as she usually did, whether he wanted to book a specific table. But he replied, "No don't call. I don't need to call to reserve a table this time. I basically wanted to go out today and if there was no table for us at the restaurant then the idea of lunch in any of the fast food places would not be a bad idea."

She was shocked by his reply and hoped, if she did not ask him, and merely went on to call the restaurant herself, to book a table for two without asking him, that she would be more certain she would have lunch in the upscale restaurant *"La Paupiette"* and not in the booth of the stalls, at a fast food kiosk.

Then, after he had noticed the shock on her face, she heard him say, "I'm only joking. But I really don't want you to call them this time, because I want to do things differently today. Anyway, I don't think the restaurant will be fully booked, especially today."

She agreed and opened the door to go out, heading towards her office. She felt pessimistic because of how she had seen people behaving today, which made her think that perhaps the restaurant would not be as ready today to receive its customers as usual. Such places usually consist of interactions between two contrasting groups, representing the two sides of social and economic life, living together in what seems to be a very rich city. It rarely sheds light on the other side of the equation, without which life could not carry on in this city, which is represented by the lesser partner in this social contract, carrying out all the tasks and services necessary for the maintenance of the rich people's lives.

It is probably the first social contract that was agreed upon between the two parties since the dawn of civilized human life, although it has not actually been signed as is the case with all other contracts. However, it managed to endure throughout the ages, and more than any other contract in the history of mankind.

She went to her office and felt that she had begun to scrutinize the sights and sounds around her, which she would normally take no notice of:

"Oh my God, why am I thinking like this now? Why is it only now that these things are crossing my mind when I didn't normally take any notice of them ever before?"

She asked herself these questions as she entered her office. Christine felt the need to sit on her desk chair for a few minutes to regain her composure, and she did not pay attention to anything else in the office. She didn't even feel the desire to check the telephone answering machine to listen to the messages. She just sat very awkwardly on the chair and couldn't relax as she had hoped.

Bob himself stood at the wide window of his office, gazing into the distance, ignoring the towering skyscrapers that tried to distract him, and which tried to make the horizon itself seem insignificant and not worth looking at.

Memories and images of his past life started to resurrect and struggle to restore his memory. They were mainly about how he had managed to succeed through his long, difficult journey, struggling and taking risks, devoted only to his work, until he had reached his current position. Indeed, he does not even consider it the pinnacle of his achievements and still feels there is more to achieve. He does not want to risk it all, so he believes that he has to constantly persevere and work hard to pursue good relationships with people whom he would not normally associate with or even want to know. Otherwise, he could face ruin. He found life tiring and boring in many respects because of all the effort, fatigue, and suffering. He reflected that his life could have been much more fun if he had not been so career orientated.

If a strong person like him, who enjoys an enviable social position as well as having great financial resources and work know how, still needs to exert further effort just to maintain their strength and prestige, when would he finally be able to feel satisfied and reassured that someone else might not dictate to him? Is that ever going to be possible? And what about the billions of vulnerable people who do not have a fraction of what he owns? How do those people feel? Bob knows a lot about such feelings. He went through several very difficult periods early in his life and remembers how often he was forced to make decisions he would never make if he were to face similar situations again today. He is fully aware that the power he gained then is what qualifies him today to do as he pleases and not feel obliged to do something he does not wish to do. But it doesn't seem to be the same thing now. Now it is becoming increasingly difficult, after all these years, and life is no longer providing reassurances to anyone. All his individual achievements could be demolished. This does not just apply to Bob himself, but anyone who has spent all of their life accomplishing things. And how much more difficult must it be for others who experience difficulties in trying to achieve things.

Apparently, it is like the deadly gladiatorial contests created by the Romans in the days of their great civilized empire, when tyranny was its main feature. Slaves were forced to fight to the death with each other for the amusement of their leaders at festivals and important celebrations. Yet in the end, the winner did not necessarily survive for long. Yes, the winner would enjoy living for a short while, maybe a few days, but, ultimately, he was dragged away to die a slow and painful death through brutal, inhumane crucifixion. Isn't this ironic, beyond ridiculous, an irony we still live with today, that after more than two thousand years, even though we pretend that we have advanced a distance on our long humanitarian journey, nothing has changed.

It is undoubtedly ironic that the state we have built cannot prevent, or, rather, does not want to care for the demise of big elephants. So why would it be interested in caring for small mice?

Isn't the suffering we endure in order to maintain what we have achieved, and our wellbeing, a modern form of crucifixion? A crucifixion of the victors, who would eventually remain hanging between the earth and the sky and don't know when they will fall.

Christine did not remain sitting for long on her office chair. She was sitting tensely, not relaxed, because she was overwhelmed by the incursion of sad, melancholy thoughts which had been monopolizing her consciousness because of what John had been talking about. However, she switched her attention to start looking forward to the coming hours, when she was hoping to escape from the horror of her nightmares, when she was going to have lunch with her employer for the first time at that upscale restaurant. She had never thought that she would one day become one of its customers. At the same time, she felt that she would not be capable of fully enjoying it as much as she should because her mind was full of the terrifying thoughts that were going around in her head, which she could not forget even for a few minutes. She didn't even feel like she wanted to get up, return to Bob's office, and set off for the restaurant even though she very much liked the idea of going there for lunch.

She turned on the answering machine, which seemed to have recorded a number of interrupted calls where callers had not left any message, which she interpreted as meaning nothing serious or urgent. But some of the company's employees, who were unable to get into work, left messages saying they might be a bit late for the same reason as she had given. She turned off the machine and felt glad that no one had left an important message, as she did not want to have to deal with anything urgent at this time. Then she remembered that she should look around the office to see who was at work and who was not. There were only four, and she did not know or care to know if there were others who might be on their lunch break. She waved her hand to greet the four who were sitting at their desks facing their computer monitors. She smiled a slight, shallow, and fleeting smile, which might not have been observed from behind the glass separating the offices from the corridor. Those who saw her waving responded in the same way, while others who didn't see her continued focusing on their computer screens and seemed indifferent to their surroundings. She took no notice because she was busy thinking of what was most important to her. Nor did she care for who was in his office and who wasn't, as she didn't know exactly what kind of work they did and whether they were supposed to be in the office or working in the field. The company's business, which is financial, economic, and investment studies, allows the employees the freedom to decide where and how they carry out their assigned studies. Each of them is given a certain period of time to do their work and the employee could spend hours or maybe even days working from home rather than actually attending the office. When they complete their project, they normally get an additional bonus on top of their usual monthly salary. This policy has been adopted by many big companies which operate in the fields of finance and economics. However, despite the fact that she was not concerned about that, and it was only out of curiosity, she still wanted to know who had and who hadn't responded to the ill fated call.

In the restaurant...

Bob and Christine exited the parking lot in his car, pulling into a street that was not as crowded as usual for a weekday. She sat beside him while he drove as planned. He did not say a thing. He still seemed to be in a state of disbelief about what he had heard from Christine, not that he thought she was lying, but in terms of what her husband wanted to do because of his belief in suicide and what it takes to actually do it. It obviously needs great strength to overcome the barrier of fear and stick to life. At the same time, a person must have deteriorated greatly psychologically and experienced a sense of defeat and frustration to contemplate it. He would never have believed it if it was not Christine who had told him. Even though the whole thing had not yet happened, and John was only in the initial stages of thinking about it, it was an explicit declaration of the rejection of life! It was a total rejection of life when life does not respond to the basic needs, wishes, and aspirations of the individual. But what are these ambitions? Would people really be ready to sacrifice their lives without achieving them? Isn't this full of meanings that mix and blend together material values with moral values? But then, isn't life the most important thing man possesses?

Christine had been quiet ever since they had entered the elevator to descend from the office to the car park in the basement of the building. Then she decided to break her silence by asking him a question which caught him by surprise after he had driven the car a short distance down the street. Her entirely surprising and unexpected question was, "Bob, do you believe in God?"

Bob did not expect such a question at all. In fact, he had never been asked this question before, or at least not as far as he could remember. People generally assume that the vast majority believe in the existence of God, in spite of the fact that people disagree with each other in terms of the importance of this God and his place in their lives, their careers, and personal behavior. But that faith is a big title that encapsulates and paints the atmosphere of society from the outside.

It was a surprise question, and he pushed his back against the car seat as if he wanted to feel stronger by supporting his back in order to be able to absorb the impact of this surprise. Before he could answer her unexpected question, he realized that his office manager was actually thinking deeply about the events. He had thought that she was only concerned about general everyday matters as most people are. Bob is also not a simple minded person, and he had an idea of what she was hinting at with her question.

He remained silent for a few moments as if he was searching through his mind to come up with an appropriate answer to this sudden question. Then he exhaled his breath from the depths of his chest before answering while keeping his eyes on the road ahead of him, "I thought I was a believer, but now I'm not so sure."

Then he turned his head to the right to look at her for a moment and then back to continue his answer, "Perhaps I should add this issue to the many other issues which I need to re examine, and to make sure that I feel sure about what I really think. I know it will not be easy and probably it would have been easier if it happened twenty years ago, or maybe more."

She responded by asking, "Why are you not sure now?"

"I don't know. Maybe because I'm not sure of many things right now! It seems to me that everything has to be re examined in order to make sure of its truth."

Christine answered, "Maybe you're right. We may have inherited a lot of things which we accept every day in our lives.

We did not create them, nor did we choose them or discover which is better when we compare them and ask which one would have been better for us? Isn't that right? In fact, we only choose a few of the things which we live by within our daily life."

He answered her with a nod, showing clear admiration for her remarks, even as he tried to keep his focus on the road ahead.

He thought to himself:

"It seems that Christine has the ability to think outside the box, which is something many people cannot achieve, although I was not aware of this before. Is this because of the strange times we are living in, or has it always existed, waiting for the opportunity to appear? It is not easy to find out, at least at this time. The answer will have to be added to the many other unanswered questions around us at the moment."

In reply she said, "If we say we really believe in God, why do you think he created us?"

Christine continued directing her question at him while still looking confused and distracted.

He answered her after a short period of silence that lasted just a few seconds, "I thought I knew that, but now I'm not so sure. I really don't know much about this, I don't know anything, and maybe we have to ask ourselves this question on a daily basis until we find a satisfying answer to it if that is possible, although I'm confused now."

"Why do you doubt it now?"

"Because I think that we should be ready to accept the results, whatever those results may be. The answer we get might not be palatable or maybe something we do not like to face. Or maybe powerful people, the elephants of this world, might not like to face the answer although weak people obviously cannot change anything in the equation of their daily lives. Since the dawn of urbanization, mankind has built their lives and laws according to what they believe. These beliefs are what created fear in them. By this I mean faith because of fear, or fear itself, is what people think is the reason for our presence in this world. I think this was one of the first principles that mankind believed in."

"Don't ask me why mankind has prioritized this terrifying matter. Even if I was certain it would be painful to state it frankly. This is particularly true if it reveals that the origin of it was nothing but nonsense based on myths invented by men thousands of years ago to explain their lives and fears. I've heard about ancient civilizations where people were keener to build houses for worship much more than they bothered about building houses for themselves. Don't you see how silly, in fact stupid, people would find it if we were to do that now?"

"Personally, I do not think the Lord needs houses where he is to be worshiped more than desperate people need homes to live in."

She did not answer the question which he added at the end of his reply, but apparently, she just continued looking ahead as if preparing to ask him another question. And soon came her question, "Do you think God loves us? I mean love all of us. I mean does he love us equally, just as I love Suzanne and Tommy? Didn't they teach us in church that we are the children of God? And that he loves us all? I am not very religious, but I know that."

He liked what he heard in her question, and he took the opportunity to inject some fun into the serious subject they had been discussing for hours and replied, "I think we should address this question to the agents of the Lord, his agents on earth! There are so many of them around, but do you know, before we ask them, we'll have to demand ID and ask them to present proof to verify their agency and to make sure that their agency, if they have any, is still valid and has not been abolished. That is, of course, if the Lord had really issued them any agency!"

"Aren't we living in the twenty first century, where one cannot claim anything without proof, otherwise he must accept whatever the consequences could be. The most likely consequence first of all would be to be indicted and taken to the court!"

Then Bob continued with a laugh, a light and gloating laugh which seemed to symbolize his disregard for someone, although it was not clear who he could be. He tried to stifle it by saying, "It is undoubtedly going to be the issue of this modern age. In fact, it is the issue of the whole of history. The fraud, the scam which has been inflicted on billions of people! People of all races, the scam which went on for thousands of years has claimed the lives of millions of people. Illegitimate agencies, based on different theological beliefs, have claimed to have been appointed by the most powerful force in the world."

As he spoke, his smile grew broader. After having warmed up to his new idea, he realized he could inject some light relief into a dark, serious topic. His smile had almost turned into laughter which he tried to stifle more than once, and then he added, "You know, there will be a lot of fun when we call those agents of the Lord and demand the documents and evidence to be validated to prove their agencies. Perhaps we should demand compensation for all the damage and insanity caused by internecine religious wars and fighting throughout history when they formed armies for their wars of people who did not understand the reality of things, nor did they know the real reason for those wars. But they were only affiliated and driven by naive motives and ignorance. Most of those wars were meaningless and corrupt. Shouldn't they be on the same side if they were honest with themselves as they claim that they are the agents of the Lord and reach an understanding with each other in a more civilized way, instead of resorting to wars throughout history which cause the death and destruction of millions of unfortunate human beings."

"Poor dear humans, we are really the sheep of the Lord. The only difference is that when we are slaughtered as a result of those wars, there will be no beneficiary of our deaths except a handful of evil people and only things that will benefit from our meat are the worms of the earth."

Finally, they reached the restaurant. Things around it were not what they usually are at this time of day. He didn't find any valet parking doormen who usually wait at the restaurant entrance to take the customers' cars to the restaurant's parking lot. He had to stop at the restaurant entrance and then got out and headed towards the entrance to see what was going on, as it was clear the restaurant was open as usual, but none of the valet parking staff were waiting outside. Christine remained sitting, waiting in the car, and did not know what to do. Bob entered the restaurant to meet the *maître'd*, Estefan, whom he knows and who was actually looking rather confused. Bob asked him why there was no valet parking service outside. Estefan apologized, faltering, and said that things were somewhat unusual today and some of the workers had not shown up. He assured Bob that he himself would take the car to the restaurant's car park.

Bob returned to the car to ask Christine to get out in order to go with him into the restaurant. She got out and joined him as they headed to the restaurant door. Inside the restaurant they had to wait for Estefan to get back from parking the car to lead them to their table. There were many unoccupied tables, and while they were waiting for Estefan, Bob invited

Christine to sit at one of the tables. He liked its location, and when Estefan returned and saw they had already chosen a table and had sat down, he went over to them and with the tone and manner of an adroit sycophantic salesman said, "Sir, you have done very well in your choice. I hope you like this table. I was going to suggest it to you."

As usual, Estefan was carrying the two food and drinks menus and began to recommend particular dishes which the restaurant was offering. He normally did this for special customers whose taste he knew well. Bob asked him not to worry about it now because they would choose anything they liked from the menu. Then Estefan said, "Excuse me sir, perhaps it's different today from other days. That is why I tried to make it easier and clearer. We haven't got everything available on the menu as usual. For instance, the meat and vegetable merchants who supply fresh produce every day could not provide our usual order. As you know, Sir, we are keen on the quality of the produce that we use for our customers. Also, two *sous chefs* who assist our Head Chef did not show up today and therefore, the Head Chef alone with others helping him in the kitchen, unfortunately, will not be able to prepare all the dishes our restaurant is known to offer and which we are famous for providing. I am very sorry, Sir, but it seems beyond our ability to control it."

Bob replied in a wondering tone, "What's going on? Why do you think the *sous chefs* did not show up today?"

Estefan answered, "Sir, it is not limited to the *sous chefs*. As you can see, many other workers didn't show up. We cannot say for sure why they didn't come in today, but it's a really serious, dangerous situation, and when you think about the reason, I really don't think I can apologize for it."

Bob interrupted him asking again, "Why do you think it's such a serious and dangerous situation?"

Estefan answered, "That's because they didn't give us a reason why they didn't come to work."

Then Bob asked him, "Do you think this has anything to do with this call? You know what I mean."

Estefan answered, "Yes, yes sir, certainly everyone knows a lot about it, but I am not one of them. (Estefan sighed as he spoke.) I know enough about it to be annoyed by it, but I don't want to be a cause of inconvenience to you, sir, or interfere with your need to have a restful, relaxing time. We will try to do what we can in this difficult time to please you."

Then he actually said that they could choose anything from the menu, forgetting either accidentally or deliberately that he couldn't provide all the dishes, and went over to some other customers who had been waiting for him to finish with Bob so that they could be served.

Bob turned to Christine, who had been listening silently to the words of Estefan, and he asked her very seriously, "Did you know it was that worrying?"

"Yes, that's why I suggested we call before we came."

"Yes, maybe we should have called, but I was not ready to change my plans because of an event like this."

"Do you mean you think it's just an unimportant thing?"

"No," said Bob, "it's certainly very serious and important, but I'm still trying to understand how it is going to affect everyday life."

"You must be kidding. How can you possibly not imagine how much this will affect daily life? I don't believe you're serious. Are you just grilling me for information?"

"No, no, maybe I didn't choose the correct expression. I myself saw many serious signs of the impact of this thing this morning, but I still think, and I could be wrong, that it won't last long, and it will not actually go on to the serious stage when people start carrying out this ultimate demand. What do you think?"

She stayed silent for a few long seconds, then her answer came, "I hope you're right and that this call does not last more than a few days, but I personally think this is not accurate. I don't want to say it is wrong because we all could be wrong when it comes to what will happen in the future. When we talk about the future, things are mere expectations, and events are therefore receptive to all possibilities."

"You're right, but I often think that such a place cannot be influenced by this kind of event. This is a place visited by people who do not complain about injustices in the world because they are the movers and shakers in the world, both in terms of the government and the way in which services are provided for everyone else."

"I think they're all happy in their jobs here, which is why I don't believe they'll contemplate ending their lives. I don't think they would support such an idea. You yourself saw it from Estefan's behavior. I've known him for many years since he started his job here..."

She interrupted him with a smile tinged with amazement, saying, "I don't know why it has only just occurred to me but you're only thinking of one side of this complex issue, and you ignore or perhaps don't care about who is representing the other sides. I'm sure you're aware that these people (and she pointed to those who were sitting at the tables behind them) assuming that he was referring to them when he said they do not complain about injustice in the world, these are not really the ones who actually affect change in the world. I'm sure they do so many things, probably more than I can count, but certainly, in order to live the lives they love, they need millions of people to provide services for them, and these are the people we do not openly see. They only move behind the scenes. Such people could be good or bad when they do things which they feel are important to them or anyone else who might be interested in inviting them or pushing them to do it."

Then he quickly interrupted her, smiling and trying to improve the atmosphere by saying, "I believe I have a communist manager in my office! But that doesn't matter as long as she refrains from frequenting places where communists might meet and she is loyal to the company where she works."

Then she replied to him, saying, "You know I'm not a communist or even a socialist, and I don't really understand much about politics or economics. I know how to manage the household budget, although it can get difficult balancing our monthly income and our expenses, and I'm not ashamed to say that I feel helpless sometimes about which things I should prioritize each month, like if there are sudden bills which I need to pay before other ones. I don't think those people (she gestured slightly, pointing at the other diners) live with the same money worries as me or other less well off people."

He interrupted her quickly at this point, "Why do you point at them when you have one of them in front of you?"

She hastened to apologize, saying, "I am sorry to have spoken like this. It was a slip of the tongue. It's not what you think."

"I didn't take it badly. You've spoken the truth. I needed to hear it from you."

And then he suddenly snapped at her, "Do you want to be like them? I mean, do you want to live their life?"

"Of course I would like to be like them. How could I be honest if I said otherwise. I think everyone like me, or maybe even people who have a bit more than me, would love to live like them. I can only explain it by saying how difficult I find it to cope with life's problems and the compromises I have to make to survive. We sacrifice a lot, a lot of what we would rather keep. Perhaps sometimes we may even sacrifice our feelings. And we always have to be happy about the sacrifice. In fact, we have to consider the sacrifice and service we offer to the others as our inevitable destiny!"

Bob asked, "Do you mean, in other words, you would like to swap places with me?"

He surprised her with this question, and she replied with a shy smile which revealed boldness and courage at the same time, "Yes, but not exactly, I still want to stay a woman!"

As she said it, she laughed louder than normal, and he also laughed with her. It was the first time they had laughed together since the morning. But then she suddenly remembered her husband and two children, and she quickly calmed down. She was also brought back to her senses by a question from Estefan the *maître'd*, wondering if they had opted for something from the menu. He directed the question to both of them, and they realized that they had not even looked at the menu. So, Bob quickly responded, "Estefan, as you have said that not everything on the menu is available today, so why don't you suggest the best of what the Chef can prepare for us. Also, please could you select a bottle of your fine wine for us."

Happy with Bob's suggestion, Estefan said, "I hope we will meet your high expectations, sir. I'll tell the chef to prepare his best dish. It will not take more than twenty minutes, perhaps half an hour at most, due to special circumstances today. The fine wine will be on your table within minutes."

There wasn't anything on this day which could be considered regular for Bob. In fact, things had not been normal since last night. The streets were empty. The hours he spent at the company were not usual. The restaurant was not the same as he expected to find it at a time like this, and most of all, Christine was not the same person at all today. He had known her since she had started working for him more than eight years ago. She was approaching her thirties when she started the same job she now holds as his personal secretary and office manager. She carried out her work seriously, consistently, and well deserved her job. But today, she seemed as if she had been hiding a great ability to scrutinize things. She did not seem to take things at face value, and she is trying to make the right choice.

These ideas kept going round in his mind while he was taking his first few sips of wine which had been brought to the table by the waiter, without him even paying any attention to who brought it. His mind wandered and was occupied with his thoughts rather than caring about all the other concerns of those around him.

Christine took advantage of Bob being distracted to use the time to look around the restaurant lounge. She gazed at various things, trying to enjoy her time as best she could and examine her surroundings, even though she was still feeling terribly stressed, which really prevented her from fully enjoying the distinctive sophistication and luxury of the restaurant. She went on to peek at the diners sitting at the other tables whenever she could. There were not many women among them, and those who were there seemed older than her. She thought that they never had to think or worry about anything serious and that none of them would suffer any of the problems that she, her husband, and children have had to face. They definitely wouldn't have to face the financial hardship she had when her husband was out of work for months. But at the same time, she was not so superficial as to imagine that these ladies did not have problems of their own, although they might seem trivial when compared to her own problems. Her feminine intuition told her that women would always be concerned about beauty and age, no matter how much money they have at their disposal.

So many questions swirled around in her mind, one after another.

That lady sitting alone at her table in the far corner looked as if she were in her mid-sixties, maybe a little older. Could she be waiting for someone to join her? I don't know, but she doesn't look like she's waiting for anyone. She's always looking at the other tables, like someone who isn't busy with anything. And she takes very small sips from her glass of wine, which has been in front of her since we arrived, without any noticeable change. We've talked about many issues, we've talked with Estefan, and she's still sitting alone. It's not difficult to see how bored she looks. Could she be a businesswoman like Bob, or is she just a rich woman passing her time here?

If it doesn't mean much to her how much this lunch must cost, then her time must also be of no value to her. How must life taste to a lady like this?

If I had some of her financial power, what would I rather be doing?

What am I saying?

How am I supposed to know how much money she has or what her financial capabilities are? How can I think about that when I don't even know her?

Bob interrupted her musing when he suddenly asked her, "Then I can assume, based on what you said, that all those who work for me would like to be in my position if they could, at least with respect to the company and its proprietors. Because it's true what you said, it's clear that it doesn't need a reason. They would be stupid if they didn't want to be in my place. Isn't that true? Isn't that what you meant?"

Christine replied, "That's not exactly what I meant. Maybe I wasn't clear or didn't choose the right words. I think it varies from person to person. Probably there are some who would like, right now, to take your position, or maybe even take it from you by force if they can. But there are also others who are grateful to you because you gave them a job at a time when there was high unemployment. However, the most important part of all this for you is that you will probably not be able to distinguish between these two groups. I think that this was what was probably on your mind, maybe not explicitly, I say *probably*."

"I don't know what I can say about this. It really isn't the most important thing on my mind right now. Do you really think that? I mean I believe I help my employees by giving them work. Isn't having a job a good reason not to envy me in my position? At least this must be true for some of them, if not all of them."

"I cannot imagine that they all harbor feelings of envy or hatred towards me. There's no reason. Maybe some of them believe that they are better at my job than I am and might think they can replace me if they get the chance."

Christine replied, "What you are doing by giving good jobs to your employees is certainly more than enough for some people, but if you even did double of what you do to help, it would not be enough for some people. They hate to see anyone who is enjoying a position better than theirs in every sense of the word."

Bob agreed, "So, this means solving the problem is not only up to me. It obviously needs a response from me, but others should get involved in order to help everybody."

She then interrupted him by saying, "I don't think it will be as easy as we might imagine. You are talking about a situation which is more akin to the situation in Plato's Republic, a fictional republic as far as I know, and according to the simple information I understand, this republic, which did not exist, maybe, most probably, will not exist."

Then he interrupted her this time by saying, "Why do you imagine that? I am only talking about cooperation between myself and the employees of the company in order to work together honestly in a genuine, friendly way for the common good..."

"If we are to speak frankly, we must say that the company is YOU! And the employees are working for you and your best interests first and foremost. The company provides them with nothing but an opportunity to work with features and advantages which differ from one to another. I hope you will forgive me for my candor. I am not one of those we meant in our words, those who represent the side of rejection or dissatisfaction. I believe you know that I am content with what

I have, and it has never occurred to me to occupy your position. Yes, it is true and undeniable that I envy you your position and your potential, but I don't want and never thought I should try to take over any of your responsibilities. Maybe another woman who has a personality and character that is different from mine might do that. I am being honest when I say that, and not just as a joke when I said I wanted to stay as a woman."

And she smiled a broad smile, but this time he did not share the smile with her. He seemed to be seriously thinking about what she had said, and then he asked her, "What do you think I can do to change the way people look at me and how can I develop and increase their cooperation with me?"

Christine replied, "I'm sorry to have brought up a subject which you've found so difficult. I am also sorry to say that you probably can't change anything. I don't think you should try to do anything to change the way people think about you. This hasn't been caused by these people or because you can't change them. It's because of who they are. They cannot provide you with any better service than they are now. I'm pretty confident that they are working to the best of their ability as far as they can. This is not based on their love to help you, but because they want to strengthen their positions in the company to achieve the rewards they anticipate. I personally think that the way things are progressing is right and fair. Maybe not the fairness and justice which many of them see as the true justice, but at least it is the best you can actually reach with them. I'm sorry I brought up this annoying issue, but you didn't really seem to be understanding it."

Bob replied, "No, it had occurred to me, but not so clearly. I'm glad you raised it. I don't know why we didn't talk about this before. Do you think I should alter my approach and try another way of dealing with the situation in the company? I don't mean my personal behavior, but administratively, so that I can deal in good faith with the employees' concerns. Do you think that could be possible?"

Christine thought for a moment and then said, "I don't know exactly because I don't think people are equal intellectually, whether you look at their thoughts, their ability, or their feelings, everything. I'm sure you feel the same. So, you can see that means I'm definitely not a communist or even a socialist. I actually believe that people are born good or evil and there isn't much you can change. Yes, you can probably change some things superficially, but you certainly can't change human genes. Aren't scientists now saying that all human features, emotions, and even their susceptibility to diseases like obesity which is afflicting people in rich nations are genetically determined? Do you think your words or a change in management style can alter the genes of the company's employees?"

Bob responded lightly, "I only wish I could change some of my genes to make myself feel less anxious and less responsible for others!"

At last, the waiter brought two large plates, each of them containing what looked like a piece of fish surrounded by a decoration of a mixture of neatly coordinated vegetables. Christine smiled when she saw it and kept looking and checking it with her eyes. Estefan was standing by the waiter to provide the explanation for the name and nature of the dish, together with all the other details related to it. He also picked up the bottle of wine to refill Bob's glass, which was almost empty. But Christine's glass was still more than half full and Bob noticed that she had not really drunk any. She said that she was not used to drinking wine at lunch time and only normally drank wine in small quantities with the evening meal when she is at home. So it is not so routine for her. Meanwhile Bob has already drunk more than half the bottle but still manages to retain his focus. Then he said, "All right, let's see what Estefan has chosen for us. Far from the literal description of this dish, let's taste what could be behind this piece of salmon and what might be special about it. I don't think I've had salmon for lunch for at least two or three years. But what's wrong with it today? Everything that is happening around us today is new, or at the very least, something I've never been used to before."

He then turned back to talk directly to Christine. She was listening to his commentary on the fish dish while holding her knife and fork in her hands. She took some of the vegetable garnish, beginning her exciting adventure with the salmon. As usual, she felt that she had to assign a certain budget to it in case she wanted to buy it from the market, although it was far more expensive than other food items. She also knew that a plate of this kind in a distinctive restaurant like this was beyond the boundaries and limits of her daily expenses. It could even exceed the pockets of all the rest of the staff who worked with her. Then Bob said, "It looks very attractive and delicious. We know what salmon tastes like, but I won't know before I taste it what new characteristic the head chef has added to its taste. Do you think these celebrity chefs who work in these high end dining establishments will be able to continue to offer more dishes that provide different tastes? Or will they stop someday because they can no longer continually innovate new dishes? Maybe they will just change the garnish or presentation without actually changing the taste."

She replied in an infinitely simple way and without hesitation, "I don't know. I must say that I am completely ignorant of the subject of cooking and the skills of these chefs in inventing new forms of cuisine. Actually, the basic raw ingredients have not changed and as far as I know, nobody has managed to add to the list of substances that people eat a new material. It's true there are people living in different parts of the world who eat substances we don't eat, or should I say we don't eat now. But perhaps we will need to eat them one day in the future."

He was listening to her with great attention as if he was meeting and speaking to her for the first time. This woman, who is middle aged, entered his service about eight years ago and, apparently, it's becoming clear to him that he is discovering new things about her which he didn't imagine. Her knowledge is general and no more than average, and what she knows has probably been picked up from watching TV. It might not have been the intention of those programs to educate people but were just shallow entertainment shows to provide general, simple, scientific information. However, if someone wants to seriously use his mind, he can easily analyze the information and form a convincing and logical argument that no one can contradict or refute.

She says that one day we might be running out of food resources and that we will actually have to eat things that we don't eat right now. It's true that we already eat food from all around the world that a hundred years ago we would never have thought of eating. Aren't we now eating strange things in exclusive Japanese sushi restaurants? These dishes include parts of creatures that we never ate before, and perhaps we never imagined that we were ever going to eat one day. This is the meeting of the cultures of different civilizations and what it brings with it. Suddenly he heard her voice directing a question to him, "Is it true what I heard of a year ago, I'm not sure when but not long ago, that a passenger plane crashed in a mountainous area covered with snow and the passengers who survived had to eat the flesh of some of the passengers who died in the accident in order to survive? Did this really happen or was it made up? Was it exaggerated and fabricated by the media?"

He replied, "Yes, it really happened, but I don't remember when or where either. I'm pretty sure that this incident actually happened somewhere in the mountains of South America. Maybe we could find out the details on Google, but I personally would rather not know about such barbaric behavior and retain a more dignified image for mankind. This whole event is absolutely disgusting, and I can't imagine that people would enjoy reading about a tragic event like this. We have become accustomed to reading about wars and killings in history as well as nowadays. We have heard about the killing of millions of people but not about humans eating the flesh of other human beings."

"Apparently we're used to reading or listening to news of murders, whether it is the killing in ordinary crimes that happen anywhere or the mass killings that happen in wars. This is mostly because we have opened our eyes and we know that wars are facts and that the murders are also facts. Murder is what necessitates fear. We have created a lot of fear inside the human soul, fear of what might happen in our lives and perhaps even more fear of what might happen after this life. This is what we see in a baby when he is afraid of strangers, even though they do not want to hurt him. He is naturally afraid of them just because he is not used to seeing them. He is never afraid of his parents and family members whom he is familiar with." "I think it's very similar to animal behavior. Ultimately fear is the main determinant of human and animal behavior. But it is we who have added another layer to it because of our constant fear of uncertainty about the future and fear of what might happen after the end of this life. Of course, animals never have to think of this. Did you know that man might be the only creature in this world who kills creatures of his own species for reasons unrelated to survival? Some of the reasons might be banal and have nothing to do with having committed a crime or offense. This occurred in historical times in many countries, including in the West. It still occurs now in countries around us when one man kills another one because of disagreements about beliefs or ideas. There are many countries which have established tough laws to severely punish those who disagree with the principles and beliefs of those who run the State, and most of those punishments are death penalties. They pronounce them without hesitation. These countries are still members of the United Nations, which is supposed to be sponsoring the principles of basic human rights. Remember that Article 18 of the Universal Declaration of Human Rights ensures the right to freedom of thought, conscience and religion."

He stopped talking for a few moments and then continued full of irony and sarcasm, "What is this conclusion I have come to? It seems as if I have let my thoughts run away with me today. This is the first time it has happened to me and confirms that today is a different day from all other days. But you did not tell me what John thinks will happen to the world if he actually carries out his threat along with everybody else who thinks it is better for them to finish their lives in this collective suicide? Oh and, as well as that, what are his beliefs? Does he believe in an afterlife which is better than this life?"

She interrupted him, wondering if he had not heard or perhaps had not bothered to respond to her question, and so went on to ask him, "Do you think it is easy for the people to eat the flesh of other people? I have heard that some remote tribes in Africa are commonly still doing so, just like some people in Asia eat monkeys and dogs! Even though I know it's really happening now, I can hardly believe that people can eat dog meat as we consider dogs to be almost like family members. And monkeys are very close to human beings, whether you believe in the theory of evolution or not."

Bob thought that she had avoided answering his question about John by returning to her former topic. He didn't push her to answer and continued with the thread, "I think it is a cultural issue linked to the time and place. If we were born in a country where its people were accustomed to cannibalism, we would certainly do the same, and if we were born in countries where its people ate monkeys and dogs, we would also do the same. We are always influenced by our predecessors. It would be very unusual for someone not to inherit cultural morals from their parents, even though they might reject them later in life. Some may believe their ways are best, however, and insist on trying to make others believe in them."

"People always imitate each other. Very few of them are able to innovate new ways and methods of doing things. Hence people often admire and are very interested in anything new, even if they were not really worth admiration. The simplest examples I can suggest would be Elvis Presley or Michael Jackson. They were from two different music and dance genres and were not preceded by anyone performing in the same style. There was about a quarter of a century between them and all those who came after who have tried to imitate either one of them failed to provide anything worth watching. This is my personal opinion, but other people may not agree with me."

He chose his words carefully and quietly. He was aware that he had suddenly been able to talk logically and philosophically. He had not been aware of this ability before. He was at the top of his game in business and trade. He understood profit and loss and was an expert on every issue to do with money and what is happening in the world of commerce, locally and globally. He had forgotten that he had previously taken time out of his normally dedicated days at work, although maybe there was only a little time to relax a bit at home. He was always working hard, juggling his attention like an army fighting on different fronts in order to build his world, represented by his business and his main company as well as the branches affiliated with it. He has only today discovered this about himself. However, he has also discovered that Christine is not only his personal secretary who takes care of his personal affairs and work connections. He knows now about the other side of her personality, which reveals a lot more information about her character and feelings, which he did not expect to discover, considering that Christine is very busy with everyday commitments and difficulties. So, what about the remaining staff who work for him and whom he talks to at some time every day, like when they have a short break when they gather in the main hall of the office to discuss business matters? He cannot remember a day without talking about work and business with his staff.

Of course, sometimes important events would take priority, such as when President Bill Clinton was questioned about his relationship with Monica Lewinski, a White House intern, or what happened on September 11th and the invasion of Afghanistan and Iraq. But most of all, there are frequent sporting events, which are the most important social events that people talk about, following their news. So, he felt that it was necessary in the coming days to devote some time to address the issues with his other employees that he and Christine had been talking about today. That would certainly make him closer to them, and most importantly of all, he would learn more and maybe discover if they had other new ideas that he didn't know. He could also identify if any of them might harbor a grudge against him. It would not be as easy as it was with Christine as he had had a long, frank, open talk with her and even now he can't say for sure what her attitude towards him is. So how long will it take him to know his staff? They will certainly be more wary than Christine. However, he knows he must have a starting point, today, tomorrow, or the day after tomorrow, he has to start from the beginning in order to get to know them better. Perhaps there could be those among them who might get along with him intellectually, which would help him understand what is going on the other side of the world, which he left behind more than a quarter of a century ago. Since he achieved his business success, which has provided him with his life of luxury, which is better than the bottom 90% of people who live their lives with various disadvantages and economic problems, he has lost touch with poor working class people. It makes him feel strange from time to time. He is still linked to those lower classes as he himself was one of them, but he feels disconnected from them. He was in contact with them basically because he needed them when he was living with them in that part of the world. But he became disconnected from them because he wanted to be part of the upper classes which dominate public life. His mind was occupied both with how he wanted to develop and improve at work as well as what he wanted to achieve as a man. He believed he should be positive with all sectors and classes of people. He believes that he has never been one of those people who carry a lot of selfishness with them and was careful not to trample on the heads and necks of others to reach his goals. Maybe that is what he was claiming in front of the others and maybe even in front of himself. He noticed once again that his thoughts had drifted far away. His thoughts returned to Christine, and he again asked her about John, "You didn't tell me anything about John. What do you think he expects to achieve from carrying out this thing he believes in? I'm sorry to say this because I still don't think he is actually serious about committing suicide, although you think he means it."

She remained silent for a few moments before she started her answer, "I didn't avoid answering your question about John as to whether he believes in life after death or not. I never avoid questions, but you surprised me and it made me realize that I don't really remember how much I really do know about it. John! Yes, John, my husband who has been living with me for more than ten years. Could this happen? Is this normal or believable? It was me who asked you: *Do you believe in God?*"

"Is it possible that life's distractions and difficulties, as well as our concerns about our children, could keep us so busy that we have stopped taking notice of each other? Could it be that I don't really know what is in his mind about this issue, even though the daily news talks about different events related to it?"

"Is this based on the faith of those who believe in this issue? Can their belief be described as a certain faith? Or does their faith bring about and dictate their behavior to them? You are right to ask your question. I need to find out more about what he believes. It is just like when he came to me believing in such a dumb call. I need to ask him for more information about it and about other things. How could a person give up something he owns now for a hope of something beyond imagination, which might come later? Isn't there a great possibility that success could be the future of our children, if we acknowledge that we have failed to achieve what we want to have in our lives?"

"Do we have the right to get ahead of the future with a stupid metaphysical prophecy suggesting that they will not be happy in their current life?"

"Whatever the foundations of this unhappy life, how could we eventually judge their future just because of a silly idea we suddenly became believers in, in a particular circumstance which has no basis and cannot be sustained?"

"I don't know why I didn't reply to him in this way or why I didn't ask him to give me a convincing answer that could really convince me of the futility of our life, just because it does not mean anything to him at the moment. As you know he has been unemployed for more than a year and he no longer has any hope of getting a job since the company has sacked hundreds of skilled workers like him in many of its plants to cope with their financial crisis."

"Yes, I have to be firm with him about this issue and shouldn't be weak. I must fight for my children and for him as well. He also needs my help now more than ever."

Then Bob interrupted her with a clear, satisfied tone, "Here is my other daughter, Christine, my older daughter, who has managed to regain her courage and strength."

Christine noticed that he had called her "my daughter!" This was reflected in the way she pushed her back against the chair more firmly. She heard him saying it for the first time and suddenly thought that she knew that his real daughter, Josephine, was only three years younger than her. He looked at her and noticed her surprise. He went on to continue, "Yes, I look on you like my daughter, Josephine. I see you more than I see her, but you don't argue with me like she does. She always contradicts me whenever I give her advice, and she doesn't seem to approve of anything her mother and I do."

"I see that as one of your generation's worst features, especially when life has always been comfortable and given them everything. Everything has always been achieved easily without effort, and this life of leisure reduces their desire to be creative. As a result, they are weak and cannot adapt to the challenges that they might face."

"I don't think it is really fair to ask her to volunteer to face difficulties in life without needing to. Other people have achieved their goals because they have faced challenges. But what is the value of any success that Josephine, or even Jonathan, might achieve?"

Christine replied, "I might be wrong, but I understand the significance of what success when facing a challenge means. A person's life will change when they have succeeded after facing a challenge. Without this change, success will have no meaning."

Bob disagreed, "Certainly not! No, I definitely don't agree with you at all. Success, when facing challenges, is character forming. It's good for the soul and strengthens self determination as well as feelings of self respect."

She quickly interrupted him, saying, "What about when failure is the result of the challenge?"

"Bob"
What about when failure is the result of the challenge??

On his way back home, Bob continued thinking deeply about Christine's sentence: *'What about when failure is the result of the challenge?'*

He didn't know until now how to analyze this sentence and how to respond. She had forced him to keep his silence as he didn't know how to reply to her, really and truly. Had he forgotten how frightened he was whenever he was about to embark on a new experience? Yes, he had overcome a lot of that fear when he became more important and achieved the power to allow him to challenge the powerful and to deal with them as equals. But he could certainly remember how frightened he was feeling in those years when he was smoking too much, one cigarette after another, whenever he was going through a difficult period. He used to wake up at midnight and couldn't get back to sleep. How could he forget those dark days?

His actual facial features, which are partly genetically determined, have been affected by his experiences. He has always sympathized with those who are vulnerable—maybe not everyone, but at least those who are close to him in his everyday life and in his work. If he was to count, look back, and relive those days, they would have been enough to transform his present pleasant days back into nightmares!

Oh my God, what bad memories do we have to live with and the nightmares they cause? We can't overcome the grief, pain, and dark memories embodied in them which keep on appearing in front of us, preventing us from measuring ourselves on a more neutral scale. Eventually, we reach the conclusion that we have committed a lot of mistakes both against ourselves and against others—maybe much, much more than that.

My Goodness, could there be someone who is satisfied with what he has and be satisfied both with his past and present? Is it possible to be assured of the future? How difficult, in fact how extremely difficult it is to satisfy the souls of some people who have these feelings!

He tried to recall, while driving, how many times in the past he had abandoned his values and principles. He did things in the past which, today, since he became powerful, he might consider to be dishonorable. Now he has the power that allows him to choose what behavior pleases him and he isn't forced to abandon the values and principles he claims to believe in and is committed to.

Yes, he can claim that he believes in these values. But it cannot be more than a claim, a claim which he couldn't uphold in the past when he was weak and in need. However, now he can translate his ethical beliefs into action and can confront others with these values which he believes are almost inherent or could claim to be genetic.

Now, one might wonder how far this behavior could stand up to a temptation of another kind. Some temptations might get him to abandon his moral principles more easily than others that seem to be more irresistible. Principles might be set aside for the chance of attaining that ultimate goal which nobody can resist, and everyone desires—the strings of power and authority! The strings of life—life, which we all want it all! Not just scattered parts of it, parts strewn here and there.

He tried to avoid those memories, which he had not recalled for years, ever since he had stripped himself of that world—the world of poor and middle-class working people. He tried to focus on the road in front of him as he drove home. The road had become very familiar to him as he had been using it for more than eight years since he relocated his office to its current address.

He tried to keep himself busy with the traffic in front of him. The streets were more crowded than they had been in the morning. But this time, some of the hints which Christine had alluded to invaded his mind when she had talked about the people who are suffering and organizing the uprisings occurring in the world. We rely on these people because of the many different jobs they do. So, this time he started to think again about the people who intend to commit mass suicide just to spite those who did not appreciate their sacrifices and needs. By "those" he means the ones who are the founders and members of the upper classes, who profit from the labors of the working class. They are the owners of the foundations, big companies, and establishments who are enjoying their life in the light of these services. Isn't it a fact that this world is devoid of justice?

Christine and John
To Meet the Difference

Christine went home after she had left the restaurant with Bob, leaving him pondering her question about what would happen if difficult circumstances in this life were challenged.

What about when failure is the result of the challenge?

She was unhappy with a lot of what she had said during her discussion with Bob. She thought that it had been inappropriate to say some of it. It might have given him the impression that she was trying to hide feelings of envy towards him. During the eight years she had spent in her work relationship with him as director of his office, she had always been extremely cautious, careful not to give him the least impression that she was anything but his most dedicated employee. She always carried out her work responsibilities to the highest level both to serve him and the interests of the company.

She knows that all employers want their staff to be relaxed, and that they make every effort to do so. Furthermore, it's also normal for them not to interfere with what is bothering their employees and what might be causing them problems in their everyday lives. In this way, they avoid being asked for help in solving their problems. However, to be fair to Bob, she thought that he had really seemed to care about this "call" for collective suicide even before he knew that John was a supporter and intended to participate in it. She was also amazed to know about, and was still surprised by, the intensity of his interest in this invitation to suicide!

This means that his interest in the topic of John is not only to please her as might have been expected. He would have had the same attitude if it were the case with another employee, rather than John, who believed in this ridiculous, frightening idea. Her discussion with Bob revealed something she didn't know about the extent of his humanity. She didn't think that employers, especially powerful ones, could be like that.

She also reflected on what she had said during their chat and decided that she had been quite brave. For a very long time, she had seen herself as someone who was non-confrontational; someone who wouldn't dare to say what they feel and what they believe in. She always did as she was told, particularly when the person giving the instructions was higher than her. But today she had discovered something about herself that she didn't know before.

She listened in the car to excerpts from the latest news about what has happened and what is happening with this "call" for suicide. Most of the news consisted of talks by analysts with contradictory views, leading to nothing but conflicting ideas. Eventually, it's clear from everything that's been said, they really don't understand anything. A lot of big events occur, their impact remains for varying periods and then they pass into oblivion before the general public knows what their facts were and people go back to their lives again as if nothing had ever happened.

So, she switched off the car radio; the sound wasn't very clear anyway. But what she understood from the news is that the general assembly or meeting, which was scheduled to be held today in the largest amusement park in the city, dispersed quickly. It's to be held at another time which hasn't yet been determined. It'll probably be tomorrow. She didn't understand why it had been postponed as people seemed determined that it would go ahead. After all commentators had given their conflicting understanding of the situation, the result was that not one of the listeners had got a sip of water to quench their thirst for reliable information.

Of course, all those commentators are the same ones who make comments on every event. How can anyone know if they are actually qualified to analyze these events? In short, how much do they really know about the foundations of these events that qualify them to step forward to explain them? The commentators are the mouthpieces of the channels employing them. The amount of misinformation and intentional disinformation they broadcast to their listeners and viewers must be huge. Intentionally or unintentionally, consciously or unconsciously, the audience has probably been misled as a result of ignorance and indifference. Also, no one knows how much the opinions and analysis could change from one hour to the next.

This is what happens in this arena where events and the media confront each other. They often play suspicious roles with motives which remain buried and secret for periods that may stretch on for a long time.

Christine arrived home. She preferred to leave the children with her mother because she wanted to take advantage of the time in the house to talk to John about the issue of this "call" without her two children being present. She didn't want them to hear their conversation as it wasn't suitable for children of their age.

She had to open the front door of the house with her key. This meant that John was not yet back home. She thought he would be late because he used public transport, and the only car they had was with her. He spent most of his time with his acquaintances, who had inspired him to take part in this stupid craze of suicide.

When she entered the house, the ideas were still going round in her head about the "call," which knocked at the doors of her thought and life. She felt obliged to follow its development because she knew she had to save herself and the children and even John, her husband, from it. But she felt exhausted and had a bundle of nerves because of the conversation she'd had for the first time with Bob. She did not know at first what to do to keep herself busy and stop thinking about the "call" until John got home. She thought about preparing some food, using what was available in the fridge to make a meal for two for when he got home. It would be appropriate to talk about the subject while having dinner, no matter what it was. She knew that her mother would take care of feeding Suzanne and Tommy, and that she need not worry about that.

She opened the refrigerator to take out what was in it, to make a vegetable salad with cold meat, which needed little preparation to get it ready for the table. She felt the silence hanging heavily over the house. There was no one with her. She was used to hearing the sound of her two children who usually filled the house with noise. So, she turned on the TV to fill the silence and to find out what was going on outside, specifically looking for news about the suicides.

The TV channel, which she always chose to listen to the news, was broadcasting a debate between a group of commentators about the event. This included the views of different organizations and representatives of various religions, who are always invited as guests to get to know their religious viewpoints on the designated event. The fake harmony was clear between the representatives of these religions, not surprisingly, as it is very easy to agree with others when everyone is keen to retain the higher ground of hypocrisy in their dealings with each other. They were fully agreed in the position they took with regards to the "call", viewing it as absolutely inexcusable behavior by any religion, and not approved of in the dogma of any religion.

They said that the possibly likely reason behind the call was not even related to religion. Religion, any religion, could offer a solution for any problem man might face. No problem should be solved with suicide! They also hypocritically agreed with each other to overlook their own differences. They were all such hypocrites! They all agreed that their religions and their representatives who Bob called "agents of the Lord" can quickly return everything back to normal, as they were. They also agreed that they could make people happy again, creating a positive outlook on life for these desperate people. They continued to share their theological theories in a very friendly, loving, compassionate, yet hypocritical way.

They forgot that they themselves normally clashed with each other and had been campaigning against each other for so many centuries. No one would ever believe that one day they would completely change and stop campaigning against their religious opponents and causing each other trouble. Nor would they believe that they would come to a peaceful understanding of life and that they would recognize each other's right to existence, acknowledging their entitlement to live and maintain their own religious point of view. Yet, each one of them thought that the other was going to hell inevitably! Each of them, in fact, represents a state of fascism and totalitarianism that is just waiting for the right time to flex its muscles and restore the historical practices which have darkened many pages of history.

Christine followed the discussion while she was cutting the vegetables, preparing the salad. She realized that, for the first time, she can differentiate between the falsehood and deceit in an interview between these "agents of the Lord". She saw through the fallacy of their arguments. This subject had now become so relevant to her due to the fact that John might join this group of suicides and his belief in their cause. Maybe, if her husband wasn't involved in the call, she might have let the TV discussion pass by unnoticed, as she usually did when important events had happened before. But this time she started to pay attention to it and also realized something else. She realized that the participants—the analysts and experts, journalists and politicians, who had come together under a common banner of secularism—actually hypocritically paid lip service to and greatly exaggerated their respect for the views of the agents of the Lord.

Despite the ridiculousness of the agents' arguments and their insignificant, meaningless responses and interpretations of the events, and how they attribute the whole reason for the "call" from the advocates of suicide is that they do not believe in a God who intervenes in the minutiae of everything that happens in this life. The Lord wanted this life to be lived this way, made up of people who are suffering, while others are celebrating; people who are serving, while others are served. She noticed that these politicians and journalists did not declare outright which side they supported. Their viewers and listeners could not learn anything beneficial from their discussion. However, it was a chance for the media to show that they could bring people together and almost revel in events as they unfold, dancing to the beat of laments and the pain of the poor. Despite this, Christine did not understand why politicians who call themselves secular, as well as the journalists, analysts and experts, tend to be hypocrites when they talk with the agents of the Lord. Why are they terrified of them, yet clearly respect their feelings?

In contrast, the agents of the Lord did not show any obvious respect for any of them, nor for their opinions. It was a difficult equation to solve. Christine couldn't really understand one part of the sum total of interpretations of these people. They came from different starting points, and everyone was trying to provide an explanation which stemmed from his actual beliefs. This was just like the agents of the Lord who were attributing the reason for phenomena like the "call" to weakness of faith. Similarly, opposition politicians believed that the reasons for this were due to the government's mistakes, while the ruling party's politicians claimed it was because the opposition party has been standing in the face of government reform, while they were attempting to address the economic situation and correct it. The same thing applies to the journalists who have to follow the will of the institutions they work for, and their political subordination, which is directly linked to their financiers.

Christine noticed that her new-found ability to criticize and discover the strengths and weaknesses of opposing points of view was not limited to the fields of politics or journalism or even limited to the agents of the Lord. This ability, in fact, works best when the critic is immersed in the situation in all its reality, rather than seeing it from outside the circle of suffering. This cannot be a substitute for suffering. Wisdom, knowledge and distinguishing right from wrong are not exclusive to the profession of living. They are open to anyone who actually lives this life.

Oh my God! What is going on? Suffering actually has creative abilities. It only needs someone who can pull the trigger to set it off. It is clear that there is a big difference between practicing and acting in life—actually living it. Suffering is what 'Wisdom' needs in order to be honest and authentic, not a fake.

Then Christine heard the sound of the door opening and knew that John had arrived. She called out: "Hello John…"

She heard no clear reply from John, who responded after he closed the door and came inside slowly towards the open kitchen door to the living room. Only then did he respond, greeting her clearly: "Hello … I don't see the kids. Where are they?"

Christine replied: "I've left them with mom. I think they need to spend some time with their grandparents. We need to talk. I'd rather be on our own without the kids interrupting."

John didn't answer her directly. He took off his jacket and threw it down on one of the chairs. His answer was a nod of the head and a contraction of his lips, grinding his teeth, as if he was contemplating what she had said. He agreed with her carefully.

It seemed very clear—his anxiety, confusion and lack of concentration. He did not seem willing to talk. He was looking for someone who would talk to him, and for him to listen, more than saying anything himself. Christine realized this and thought it was encouraging. She felt that there was a chance whereby she might be able to start to remove the idea, the nightmare, of suicide from his mind. It was as if he was looking for a way out of the psychological crisis that surrounded him and prevented him from enjoying anything to the slightest degree.

He was like someone who had just discovered a sad, painful, devastating, disheartening fact, something which suffocated any desire to carry on living, despite any love for life or attachment to it. Life had finally turned its back on him, and overnight he started to feel he had failed at everything at every level. It is a really devastating, killing feeling. It's no surprise, then, that all of this would start to make him feel like responding when he heard the "call".

Christine said: "Dinner will be ready in minutes. I'm sure you're hungry. Did you eat something before you left this morning?"

John responded: "I only had my usual coffee. I didn't feel like eating anything else."

Christine said: "I took the kids to school this morning, and when I didn't find any members of staff there letting the children in, I thought I'd take them to my mom. There were many other parents waiting in front of the school door in a quandary, not knowing what to do. If mom had not been available, or if she'd had other plans, I would have been in the same situation, and I couldn't have gone to work."

She then recounted to him some of the things that had happened to her in the morning, while she was placing the dishes on the dining table. She watched his face to see how her words were affecting him. As he was listening to her, he sat down on a chair in the living room, trying to relax. He listened to what she was saying without looking at her, but, apparently, he was still concerned about the kids as much as he had been before this ill-fated "call" had taken place which had come between them. He said: "Then, you managed to go to the office today. How did things turn out there?"

"Things weren't the same as usual. I didn't feel the same in the morning as I do now."

She wanted to turn his attention by the second part of her answer to the fact that the way she was in the morning had changed and that she felt different now. She was waiting to see whether he was paying attention to what she had just said and how much he was focusing his thoughts on her and how much her words meant to him.

He waited for a few moments after she had finished her answer, to reply in a questioning tone: "I understand that things were not the same as usual. That's what I would expect. But I don't understand what could change you between the morning and now?"

She was pleased to hear him inquiring about this, and she had finished the preparation of putting the food on the table. She went on in her answer after she invited him to sit at the table, by saying: "You're right. Maybe I can't clearly say what's changed from the morning until now. The right words don't come easily to me. I might not be describing it accurately, but I think I've started to see a lot of things that I didn't use to see or notice before, both in myself and in others."

"…And what was it that led you to see things today that you couldn't see before? I don't understand what you mean. How did this happen? Why today in particular?"

He stopped his rapid questions, waiting for her answers, while looking at the food in the dish in front of him, slowly tasting it, but not showing much interest in it. She also stopped, and looked at him for a few moments, then answered: "Today was unusual both in the office and outside. Everything was unusual. In fact, today wasn't really an actual working day. I could say it was a day of getting to know myself and other people as well."

She stopped again, waiting for his reaction to what she had said. John stopped looking at his plate and turned to look at her, asking her in a wondering tone: "Getting to know others—who are the others?"

He stopped asking—waiting for her answer which was slow in coming. After a few moments, which felt like a long time for him, she answered him: "Not many—in fact only one—it's Bob. You know Bob, my employer."

John stayed silent waiting for more clarification. She continued: "I learned something about him today. He has qualities that I didn't expect him to have. I used to see him as a person who didn't know, or care, about anything apart from being serious and controlling his life—both his work life and his home life, it doesn't matter which, because it seemed to me as if they were the same thing and had the same value for him. One wasn't worth anything without the other. They stand side by side with each other. Just today I learned a lot about his feelings that he had never revealed before. Maybe I'm the only one who works for him who knows this about him."

John remained silent, waiting for Christine to reach the heart of the subject, because he knew that what she had said about Bob was not what she meant by: 'I didn't feel the same in the morning as I do now.' However, she deliberately went silent for a few moments. Perhaps John would say something or ask her to finish what she was saying. But he didn't and remained silent, waiting for her to carry on talking about what had happened to her that day. When the silence became uncomfortable she felt she had to carry on talking to stop John losing interest in it and changing the subject. She felt it was better for her to talk about what had happened between her and Bob and try to get John involved as much as possible in the talk, even if it was through his questions. So, she carried on:

"When I got to the office today, I was, as you would expect, extremely agitated and upset, after everything we'd been talking about last night, as well as the conditions that I had gone through in the morning with the children's school, and I had to take them to my mother's home. When I got to the office I found Bob waiting for me eagerly, not because I was late, which is what I thought to start with, but because he was apparently busy thinking about the "call". We were busy with it, even though it doesn't concern him as much. However, he was very interested in finding out everything about it and was thinking deeply about the reasons that could be behind it as well as the people who are calling for it."

John was listening to Christine attentively, furrowing his eyebrows expressing a level of focus and interest in her words. But he was surprised at the same time about how interested Bob was displaying this mass suicide. So, he interrupted her, wondering: "Does he know anyone who intends to participate in the call?"

She quickly answered him and emphatically denied his question saying: "No, no, certainly not—he was surprised that the "call" had gone out and how serious it was. All he knows is what he has heard from television news channels. He was trying to find out information in addition to what is on the TV from what he could see around him and through questioning me."

"Questioning you? What did he ask you? Why is he asking you anything?"

"Actually, he was not asking me," Christine continued. "But he noticed how upset and confused I was this morning. That was why he kept on asking me to explain why I was so upset. There was no escape. I had to talk to him about why you are determined to follow the 'call.' And I needed to talk about it with anyone who would give me a chance. I think I talked to the best person I could have and the result was that I felt in the end I had made remarkable progress in my ability to notice things around me, or at least that's what I thought. It was very useful to help me explain different things. Perhaps this 'call' for suicide is one of them. I say 'perhaps' because I still don't understand this 'call' and I'm waiting for you to explain it to me, that is if you have any information you trust and believe."

"...Perhaps you could say what more you knew about Bob today, that you didn't know before?" John asked.

Christine answered: "...I know he is a man who cares about the people around him, not based on how much use they can be to him financially. I know he is interested in the conditions of the people and wants what is best for them, even if that does not have a positive effect on his life. I know he is happy not just because he is strong financially. It was important for me to know this, to be convinced and believe him, because you hear a lot about it—I mean the impact of money on people and how they behave. Maybe I've just learned this from stories, from fiction. But, actually, I also discovered something about myself. I've realized that I can reach convincing results, or at least fairly reasonable results when I seriously think in a particular subject. In the past I thought that I didn't have the mental ability to explore serious issues that require uncompromising thinking, and challenge commonly-held beliefs."

"Like what?" John spoke sharply. He wanted an answer. He remained staring at her, waiting for her to say something. But she bowed her head and turned to eat something from her plate in order to give herself breathing space so that she could answer him. After a few seconds of silence, she answered:

"I've learned that I have the ability to analyze things independently and that I'm not a follower of what other people want—or believe in what they believe in. I have learned that I can rely on my own convictions and not those of other people like my parents and grandparents. I don't think I could have done this without talking to Bob. My talk with him was not only the most important, but unusual thing also to have happened to me today, it's the most important thing that has ever happened to me. He also invited me to have lunch with him in his favorite restaurant, because he wanted to find out more about how he could help us in our present situation."

"He invited you to lunch. How did that happen? What was the reason?"

Christine explained: "Yes, he wanted to find out about the call to suicide especially when I told him that you are committed to it. He wanted to know more because he only heard about it for the first time about two days ago on the television and in newspapers. I saw him very differently today from the person I thought he was. I learned that not everything we view as bad actually is bad."

John replied: "It seems like your day was really unusual. It was busy, and certainly useful to you. It certainly wasn't like my day. It was as if it was wrapped in darkness. I couldn't see anything through it. That darkness increased my confusion and hatred for life, and everything that is going on in it. I particularly hate those figures of great importance and anyone who represents them, who controls life. I even hate myself. I'm not prepared to think about it anymore, not the old life which I loved, or the new one, which I'm trying to be an active part of. At least that's what I imagined I believed in my naivety and superficial understanding of the issues."

"I can't pretend that I am able to resist this desperate obsession which is knocking on my door. It is as if all my doors and windows have been thrown wide open to a foul cold wind at one time and a flame from hell at another time. I don't even know what hell is! What am I talking about? I don't understand these questions and beliefs. I don't know if they really exist, or if we are so used to them having a role of the ultimate absurdity in our lives, which, in turn, is the most ridiculous part of absurdity. I'm absolutely exhausted; I'm desperate; I've collapsed; I don't want to hear anything; I don't want to know anything. Everything I was sure of in my life, for more than thirty years of my conscious existence have not helped me in any way at this desperate time."

"Where is the Lord they are talking about?" "Where is his fairness and justice?" "Where is his mercy?" "Everything is a fantasy, an illusion, published and distributed by the powerful among the powerless. Those who have the power know what to do, and those who are powerless don't know what they are doing. They don't know what kind of illusion and absurdity they are living in. They are nothing more than puppets in the hands of the powerful."

"Life is just a game and there is a gang of powerful arrogant men who play it the way they like. There is no reason to participate in playing this game, just to delight the powerful to entertain them."

"This is what I have to say to you and Bob. I don't know what topic you discussed. It might have interested me if it had happened two weeks ago—or maybe even a week! But it's no longer significant now. Things have become clear to me—things of another kind—not what you think you have learned about today."

Bob and His Family Gather

The return of Bob to his home was not the usual schedule, and his wife, Nicola, was waiting for him. He called her on his way to the house, and she told him that their children, Jonathan and Josephine, were coming today for dinner with them. They had planned this date a few days ago, but it seemed that Bob had forgotten about it in the midst of these unusual events. Jonathan was travelling on business to several other states, and now that he was coming home, dinner was going to be a family gathering.

Bob arrived before the arrival of Jonathan and Josephine and was apparently eager to see his three grandchildren: Jonathan's son, Steve, who was four years old, and Josephine's son and daughter, Carol and Ted, who were eight and five years of age.

Nicola received him with a joyful smile and a kiss. She was busy preparing food, assisted by her two housemaids, who were of South American origin. Thousands of people were infiltrating the different southern states. They were mostly illegal migrants seeking work for low wages.

Bob knew that the extraordinary welcome Nicola gave was also due to the fact that she was preparing dinner for their son, daughter, and grandchildren. It was only natural, and maybe it could be enough to overcome the pain and bitterness that both Bob and Nicola had been feeling while they had been listening to the depressing news and feeling submerged under the suffocating atmosphere that had been around for the last three days. The few hours with their children and grandchildren would give them a short break.

Oh my God, how selfish man can be! He is selfish in himself and all of his feelings. Could it be that one day, man will overcome his selfishness, or is it an animal trait that cannot and will never change? He will never overcome it… never!

Josephine came in with Carol and Ted, her two kids. Her husband, Ernie, works evening shifts, so he wasn't there that day. He is a technician with a waste recycling firm. Bob embraced his granddaughter, Carol, who was always throwing herself into his lap to get his attention. She did this to stop him from embracing her brother and to keep all his interest. Bob didn't like to interfere with her attempt and tried to reassure her by keeping her in his arms, while reaching out to his little grandson, Ted, to encourage him and pull him gently to him to cuddle him with his sister. After a few minutes, he released them to devote himself to his daughter. After hugging her mother when she first came in, Josephine came over to hug and kiss her father.

Bob asked Josephine about her life and how things were going with her husband and children. She took her children by the hand to the family room so that she could show them where their toys were kept in their grandparents' house. Bob was not expecting his daughter to know much about what was going on with the "call" for suicide, so he didn't ask her about it in particular. He thought that perhaps her husband knew a lot about the "call," but that he didn't discuss such topics with her. She's always busy with her children and doesn't appear to care for anything outside of this little cocoon. She's not interested in what's going on in the world, or even around her, unless it's directly related to her. She's like millions of people who don't have any interest in anything outside of their personal lives or what touches them directly. These people don't feel the flames before they start burning their clothes. This is why, when he talked about her to Christine, he didn't show how he felt when he mentioned the way she behaved with him and her mother.

Jonathan arrived with his wife, Liz, and his son, Steve, shortly after the arrival of his sister. It was clear from the warm, eager way that Bob welcomed his son that their relationship was very close, which was a big contrast with how he behaved when Josephine arrived.

Nicola hugged Liz affectionately, then picked up her grandson in her arms, giving him a warm, loving hug. She then embraced her son and asked him about his trip and how it was, while Bob hugged his son's wife in greeting and then went on to embrace his grandson, who hugged him in return, clearly showing how much he loved his grandfather. Jonathan went over to greet his father and embrace him. Bob asked him about his trip and whether the results were feasible. Jonathan answered that it wasn't bad, but it didn't bring him the results he was hoping for. Then Jonathan returned and, before sitting down, he surprised Bob with a question about that subject with which his father's mind had been busy, the "call" for suicide, as if he knew that his father must have been thinking about this subject. He knew that his father was always greatly interested in things like this and always considered such matters from all sides comprehensively. He was never narrow-minded in his thinking.

John's questions showed that he wanted to understand his father's point of view about the "call." He wanted to know what good it might do and what impact it would have on the future. It was not like other "calls" that had preceded it, which were limited to the scope of narrow sectarian religious groups that had emerged between very restricted groups of people. Afterwards, they committed suicide collectively in different ways. These "calls" did not cause any kind of impact on society, and no one really remembered them after they were over. Bob approved of Jonathan's question, which clearly revealed his worry and distress about the "call." It showed that he treated it as a matter of utmost importance that should concern everyone living in their country. This particularly applies to those who want to create their own business, whatever the form or nature of that business. In the beginning, Bob wanted to question Jonathan about how much he knew about the call, but Jonathan pushed his father with his question. Bob was momentarily speechless and didn't know how to answer. Moments later, he answered, "I think I must say, above all, that this 'invitation to suicide' is very serious. That's how it seems to me. It's very important that the community gives it the attention it deserves. This is not like previous 'calls,' and I don't think those other calls relied on the same depth and seriousness. More importantly, I don't think any of those calls stemmed directly from the hearts and souls of the people who were really suffering. Anyway, you tell me, what do you know about it?"

Jonathan answered, "I don't know anything more than what the media are saying, and what some people are saying…"

"What are people saying?"

"Not much. I don't really know any of them personally. But it seems that there are probably thousands of them who support it. I know two of my colleagues at work who obviously have relatives and friends who are actually convinced by it. They've reached a state of utmost despair and might participate in it. As you say, it seems to be a serious and unusual invitation."

Bob replied, "Yes, but it certainly doesn't seem like the authorities think the same way; otherwise, they wouldn't have left it this way without it being reported properly so that people know the truth behind it. The reasons behind this 'call' will continue to exist as long as human beings live on the earth. Even if their problems are dealt with, something else will reappear after a few years and will carry on appearing and disappearing. This is proved by the cases of the dictatorial and fascist ideologies which we have lived in many incarnations in the last century."

Then Jonathan interrupted him suddenly, by saying, "Dad, I didn't know you were so interested in politics. What you've said might be true, but, at the same time, I think they either don't want to ascribe too much importance to it so as not to disrupt work and everyday life, or, and this is what I really think, they probably do not know how to handle and resolve this type of situation. It's unprecedented, and it doesn't seem to matter who participates in it. We all know that suicide is an individual choice. It's a personal choice. People have the right to choose it, especially in a country that considers itself to be the only truly democratic country in the world."

Bob answered, "Mmm… I'm really happy to know you're thinking this way. You don't seem to let events in the news pass you by unnoticed. These events have to be dealt with very seriously, particularly by people who want to develop their business. Now, tell me how your trip was and what was the purpose of it?"

Jonathan replied, "It was for two purposes. First, to find a market for the new program, which we're preparing, and, secondly, to interview some technicians and experts who might be able to participate in our future projects. The trip wasn't successful and not as productive as we needed. But I didn't expect much better results. The recession is still hitting most aspects of my work hard. There's a surplus of IT engineers. Everyone wants to develop their designs, but their ideas are very similar, and there is strong competition. Other parts of the world are doing a lot of what we do, but at much less cost. The golden age of the giant information technology empires and computer software companies has now passed."

"Do you think this is going to threaten your future and the work of your company?"

"Yes, to a certain extent. Actually, it will probably have an impact on everyone."

Bob continued, "I don't know of anyone who hasn't got problems at work. Even those who produce food are complaining about their difficulties and lack of state support. Humans can't live without food. Indeed, they desperately need more in many countries of the world. Prices have fallen so low that the farmers are unable to cover their costs. I think we pay double for our food than what we used to. Yet half of the world's population is hungry. Isn't this a strange equation? Sometimes, I would love, if I could, to put myself into the shoes of one of those who call for suicide just to know exactly what could make a man ready to decide to end his life. I'd like to know that because I feel the world is moving inexorably towards a dangerous destination. Its end will probably be in this destination. The world, as we know it, will end. Many people throughout history have tried their best to make it a safe world and not let it get as dangerous as it is now. While there are many people serving the interests of humanity, there are just as many others who want to carry out its destruction. They want to destroy everything that has been built by the hard work of generations through centuries of determination and struggle."

Jonathan said quickly, "You mean the politicians and rulers, who are controlling the world."

Bob agreed, "Look at that. What a wonderful conclusion. I really feel you are my darling son. I don't need to worry about you as I used to."

Jonathan smiled, "Don't forget, Dad, I inherited my genes from you. I learned a lot of my ideas from you, directly or indirectly, from my upbringing. I think I was a good student."

Then Nicola could be heard, calling them to come to the table for dinner.

Christine and John

The atmosphere of sadness and melancholy shadow remained clouded over the living room where Christine sat, moiety of mind, devoid of any desire to do anything, as she sat in front of John, who himself also sat semi-collapsed after he let out some of what was in his chest of the sense of weakness and collapse. Perhaps he still had a lot of what he said still hiding in his chest, but he did not mean to address it to Christine, whom he loved and still loved, and loved his children. But how much he wished to have the opportunity to vomit what was inside his gut in the faces of those who direct and control the "game of life," this game that had become boring for anyone who has senses, for those who are living on the margin of life, a game that increases its disgusting routine and depression as much as the happiness of those who control and move it increases.

His words about his feelings brought Christine back to square one, where she was in the morning when she was without any ability to control what she should do, or think that doing it was the right thing.

Is it possible that what John is saying and feels is the truth which everyone is trying to evade?

If his feeling is not correct and not true, then how could we explain what is going on in this world of injustice passing in front of our eyes and we are unconcerned with it, as long as it did not slap us in our face?

Here it slaps; in fact, it crushed thousands, perhaps millions of people around the world, where the hands of the influential controllers easily reach out when they want to do so, and at other times, the hands of "the Lord," who seems to have sympathy with those influential controllers, would do the same work on their behalf.

Could it be he is only "the Lord" of the influential controllers, and not "the Lord" of everybody?!

And is it thus that he tries to evacuate the atmosphere as much as possible for the influential?

Could this be what happened and is happening through the ages?

Christine regained her consciousness and attention after a period of heavy and dark-colored silence, which overshadowed the atmosphere between her and John. Then she got up and went to the kitchen to make coffee, and she recovered some of her strength while preparing it. Without her seeing John, or him seeing her where he remained in his place, she said aloud so that he could hear her, "I think we have to seriously think, and without emotions, about what is happening!"

No response came back to her from him. He remained silent. Then she returned to continue what she was saying, "I also believe we must think about our children more than we think of ourselves, and not limit ourselves to speaking about the negatives in our lives. We have had many times, and we still remember how much joy we've had and how comfortably we were living."

John continued in his silence and didn't respond to what she said, and therefore she was encouraged to say more:

"We know nothing about those who are calling us to 'die' and to end our lives by our choice, and I have the right to wonder. You also may have wondered about the significance of this 'call.' We do not know who is behind it. Isn't it possible that those influentials could be behind it, maybe some of the minds who innovate investment plans and ideas, and see in the death of people of this class what could bring more benefits to them? Almost the same as what is seen by these desperate advocates of this 'call,' who intend to hurt the influential by killing themselves! I don't know, I don't know. I would like to hear anything more about them from you. What do you know about them to have this trust in them? What do you see in them to have this satisfaction in yourself in what they are intending to do? Would you have been convinced by their 'call' if you were still keeping your job, the job which you loved?"

Here came the voice of John quietly answering her, "It is not important to know who they are and what the details of their real motives are. What is important is that it has opened my eyes to the vanity and futility of this life, when I only stay alive consuming food which has become the business and trade of those superior influential controllers of life, who benefit from its gains and revenue more than the farmers and workers who actually produce it could ever get. Only this is enough to keep me for hours thinking to find out how unjust this life is, and how we ourselves, the inferior, are involved in deepening the roots of injustice, and how much we contribute to filling the bellies of these superiors with our hard work and effort."

"But we cannot solve this dilemma by choosing to leave life by ourselves. There must be another way to settle the matter and to reach satisfaction and self-conviction."

"Yes, yes, it is possible. We can continue to deceive ourselves and continue to live in the shadows of stupid, flimsy hopes and aspirations…"

"I don't care what it could be, whether it is deception or not. I will be in this situation as pragmatic and realistic as possible and will not care for anything but you and my children, even if that requires me to fight whoever it is, whether owners of big companies, members of Congress, or all the governors of the world!"

John did not answer her in reply to what she said, but he remained silent, looking without focusing on anything in front of him. She felt that her last words, when she summed up that she cared about nothing but protecting him and her children, had been received with welcome and found a place within him. Perhaps she had inspired him by choosing war against the influential and not intending to accommodate or acquiesce to their wishes. That was something that raised his interest and attention and possibly pushed him to think about an alternative to suicide.

But which alternative?

Big TV Dialogue

A major media TV channel organized a special discussion meeting to cover this great and unique event of its kind, as it is the first event that provides media devices the opportunity to be covered and to talk about it before it happens, and not afterwards. Although no one knows exactly when it will happen, or rather when it will start happening, since it is supposed, and according to the public information received about it, it will happen consecutively in the states and cities, in several different locations, and probably will happen in homes or public places. Several figures of media and some others who call themselves political analysts were participating in this discussion; also there were sociologists and psychiatrists and politicians from different parties and orientations of conservatives and liberals.

The host of this discussion meeting also opened the opportunity for a good number of the public, who were interested to participate as audience only, and some of them probably will have the opportunity to raise some general points related to this event, to represent the viewpoint of the man on the street. Also were invited to this meeting, representatives of the common different religions in the country who represent more than a church, and representatives of the Muslim community of both the Sunnis and Shiites sects, and one representative of the Judaism religion. There was one of the participants through the TV phone who represents one of the atheistic organizations, who is a well-known space physics scientist.

The meeting place was in a large hall, and the cameras at the beginning of the meeting were focusing on the host of the meeting, who is a well-known media figure, and often has a first round in the coverage of the important events like this. He started his speaking about this "call", and described it as the first call in history to call people to commit suicide collectively and without a clear reason as to why they call for the committing of this suicide?

But, there is a scheme which may, or may not achieve its objective, which is creating a big chaos and crises to the rich, high-end class people who need different services, those services which are provided by the middle and poor classes of the society. The high-end class people are the owners and investors of these services businesses, and not the actual workers in these services! They are the business owners and the employers who rely on labor from other classes in their business and their investments; it is meant to create a crisis for them and threaten to obstruct and stop their business and their interests, maybe for a long time!

Also, he stated that this "call" has emerged and spread its news among the people through the social media in the beginning, then the media channels began its coverage through simple information available. Though the people who were involved in discussion and talking through the means of the social media were not more than a few hundred, it seems that many of them do not wish until this time to reveal their position in this "call" and to announce whether they actually will participate in it as "suicidal", or they will only remain supporters and calling only the others to carry it out on their behalf!

Then he raised an important query point, which is: **Whether this "call" represents a protest stance on people's living conditions, or it actually really means to embarrass the giants of the rich people when their business machines and process stop, completely or partially?**

There was also the assembly place point, which has been called by the advocates of this "call" who did not reveal themselves and their identity until now, which indicated that the assumed assembly meeting is to take place in a site in the big city, which is the largest public park where people go for walking or sporting their activities like jogging, cycling, walking or sitting. This assembly meeting, which has not accomplished today more than it experienced a noticeable, significant and unusual increase in number of people who were there, but it was not known whether those people are those who actually will participate in this call, or support it, or that many of them were only those who are curious and hoping to see what could happen?

Then the host started to present the participants in this dialogue meeting and stated their names, which obviously he himself didn't know some of them, and therefore, he had to read their names from a list he carried in his hand. After having finished reading the list, he returned to talk about the topic of suicide, and said he would ask the guest of the meeting, a specialist in psychiatry to shed light on the suicide process in general, what forms and what motives lead to it.

The psychiatric specialist guest answered by saying: "The suicidal behavior is a resort to a haunted person who experience bouts of psychiatric disorders such as an extreme depression or frustration, or a feeling of total despair, or when falls under the influence of drugs used to treat mental illness, when one of the side effects can push their users to suicide. In all these cases, for those who commit suicide, they have to be under the influence of one of these factors or situations, or more than one factor at the same time, and it is clear that all of them do not apply to what we have today of the status of general advocacy for collective suicide carried out by people who do not seem to have a health problem or have something which (according to Psychiatric Medicine) calls for suicide. But it is possible, and this is very likely, they could be severely frustrated psychologically, and this is what can be mostly a common phenomenon spreads, and causing severe depression among the people."

The comment of the host of the meeting after he interrupted the Psychiatrist was: "Does this mean we are facing a new cause for suicide to be added to the reasons that are already known to psychiatry as reasons for suicide?"

"I can't say that, because we have nothing but little information about the people who advocate for this "call" or its participants, or at least I can't say that I am sure of my information about the reason for this "call" for collective suicide, and we need to know a lot of its details before we can give it a correct scientific psychological explanation."

"Then, let us ask the specialists of information about the extent of their knowledge of this (call), and the question is also directed to anyone who has a definite and reliable information about this "call"."

Here, one of the media figures who represents a conservative media allied to the Conservative Party, which represents most of the owners of capital and production tools in the country said: "We know nothing but very little of reliable information about those who are activists and enthusiasts to this "call", and this has been mostly formed through the use of social media driven by youth often, these young people are motivated by many motives, mostly chaotic and not based on the reality which we live in."

And here, one of the attendants representing the liberal media interrupted him by saying: "This is an unfair abstraction of the facts; it is clear that these people are suffering from difficult economic conditions which brought them to a more difficult social situation, creating in them this frustration feeling to the point of the toughest choice option, which is to end their lives. We must not always underestimate things and events, and leave them without taking the required care because they do not directly concern us, until we one day suddenly get the surprise when they impose on our lives what we can't get rid of its nightmares. There is an important question everyone should ask, it is: Why didn't the general strike be the alternative to suicide?

I think I can contribute to the answer without neglecting the answers of the others, and so I think that the choice of suicide strike was the result that those who advocated this "call" wanted to deliver a stronger message this time. The message is that they do not want to compromise this time on this issue, by lifting wages which may not fit the level of the rise in the cost of living, and then back again to the need of another strike which may or may not bring a good result that satisfies the working class?"

The host interrupted him by asking: "This question is realistic and logical; maybe too many of us didn't pay attention to it, but could you tell us what do you know about this "call" and those who advocate for it? Does this "call" mean that the culture of suicide is to be common in the societies worldwide?"

"I know there are students who excel in their studies, and descended from poor families working in the simple service needed by everyone. They are not reassured that they will be able to complete their studies, nor are they able to provide the necessary health services for themselves and for their families. I know many people who work and cannot save what they need as a down payment to buy a small simple house; I know some of them living on unemployment benefits for nearly a year or more.

Maybe what we need at this time is to go through the inner streets of the city which we don't think in going into them, and we do not know what goes inside there. Maybe someone would say that the roads and fields are open for these aspiring young to reach advanced positions in their practical real life, making them perhaps the leaders of the country, but whoever says that must not forget that there has been no one who managed to achieve this thing without attribution and support of a strong hand, financially or politically. The support and attribution of the political parties and big companies should be assigned for those who want to reach a high position in the future, and without this they should not dream of it! Unless they were those who invent devices or inventions which open up the appetite of the big investors, or authoritarian companies which control and lead the economies of the world!"

One of the politicians of the ruling party took the initiative to reply to him: "This case, I mean the economic recession or any case like it, almost prevails in the whole world and not confined to our country. The government has inherited a heavy load from its predecessor, and the economy in all countries of the world is suffering from difficulties in different forms and degrees, and we all suffer as a result of the suffering of economy."

The host intervenes, in a wondering tone: "And what do you think has changed between the current government and the government preceded it? Unemployment is still the same, and nothing has changed in health care, but some say it has become more difficult for those who have the insurance, and those who don't have it are in worse situations. Health care costs and wages of doctors, hospitals and the cost of drugs increased rapidly, and insurance forms in general have become elusive for many people, especially the old age people, and the government is promising a lot of things and could not fulfill its promises. There is a feeling among the people that the government spends a lot of money on external affairs which do not benefit the citizens in any actual way, but rather are in favor of big companies, and most major companies are investing in other countries, and the unemployment is growing in the country. Let's go back to our theme of those who advocate for the suicide, to ask how we can stop such a "call" to preserve the lives of people who intend to kill themselves, and the question is to all of you."

The conservative media representative intervenes at this point to say: "It is certain that this issue has deep roots, we cannot lose sight of or denounce it, but at the same time, it can't be a solution to the problem of the working class, and therefore, it is very important that we don't give it what is greater than its size of importance, and consider that it would be the end, and everyone will choose to end his life this way."

Then a liberal media figure interrupted him by saying: "It is this attitude which is scary! We are afraid that the governments never move before disasters strike, and I mean the disasters which we are causing most of them, like disasters caused by our impact on the environment due to the abuse of all forms of energy, and this "call", which will be a disaster preceding other disasters which will follow if we do not act on the knowledge of its causes, and to be serious about finding solutions to them."

Then the host interrupted him to ask the Christian preacher about what it deems necessary to contribute in a stance to stop such a "call", especially since religions never approve killing oneself?

The Preacher answered, saying: "This event is not to be considered unusual, especially when we have transformed our lives to make it a theatre and a market of materialistic needs, and a vacuum of spirituality, and moved away from the Lord and the needs to be close to him, and not to behave the way he did not tell us to do. The Lord has commanded us to love others and do not look to what they are enjoying and what is in their hands. If we were deprived of anything in our lives, we should not look to our deprivation as it is something will be forever, but it will disappear just like all the suffering, disadvantages, obstacles and the difficulties we face in our lives!"

Then the liberal journalist intervenes in a clear condemnation tone and said: "But hey (Father) these people are not asking for things of luxury, they ask for their rights of education and health care, and I think you recognize these as their rights, and they deserve that their children not to be exposed to severe poverty, which drives them to slip to commit crimes. And I must say I did not know what are the disadvantages and the difficulties and the suffering that must eventually disappear from our lives? What about those who have been born in the bosom of disadvantages and difficulties and poverty, and they live there up to their death,, not to mention those people who are born with disabilities, who will need special care and assistance from the others throughout their lives?"

Here, the Shiite cleric decided to intervene, saying: "Yes, much of what you say is true, but the (Rev. Father) meant that man should not lose hope and that he should know that God divides the livelihoods by his will between the people to keep life going through mutual benefit. So the objection to invalid system is not to be taken by suicidal, but it is to challenge it first by the peaceful means, but if it did not work, it can then be by a revolt erupted as our Imam (Husain) on the bias and injustice State!"

Here comes the time when the Sunni cleric decided to participate after the Shiite cleric stormed the debate,, and he said without introduction, as if he is lecturing the public spectators while in a mosque a religious jurisprudential lecture: "There are a lot of lessons that we can inspire of Islam in its state, where Islam maintains Justice which makes the citizen voice heard by the Muslim ruler, no matter what the state of this Muslim citizen and his class in the Muslim community, and for us in the State of Islam in the first caliphate what may could maintain justice in the whole world, and without falling into disobedience to the Creator!"

The host interrupted him by saying: "Sorry to interrupt you Sir, but we have with us over the phone the professor of cosmic physics whom we would like him to share with us the discussion of this issue as he represents the opposite direction of the spiritual faith trends, yes, go ahead professor:"

"Thank you for giving me the opportunity to participate and comment about this issue. I could not put up ways to handle this situation because I know that this is not my specialty, and the problem is not of one origin, nor of one kind; it is deeply rooted in the society, and needs a group of specialists in economics, humanities and social sciences. But I have at this time questions to the respected gentlemen who represent faith and spiritual faith side in their suggestive treatments for such problems. My first question is to the Rev. Father: Can spiritual therapy provide health services to the family which does not hold a health insurance, or help when its breadwinner has been unemployed for a period of more than one year?

And to the Shiite Sheikh, I would like to ask him if he wants these people to rise up and revolt like his Imam (Husain), while I myself as far as I know, the people who are the followers of (Husain), in the land where (Husain) was murdered, which is Iraq today, those people have not been able to revolt against their governments, or even raising their voices, in follow up of the footsteps of their Imam, imitating what (Husain) himself did. And if I may ask him and the others who are concerned: Where could their revolt take them against the violence of the dictatorship States, and the suppression in many parts of the world? And the news of Iraq says that Husain's followers of Shiite sector, who are ruling Iraq now, they did not care or pay the least attention to serve their followers, nor they did any good but for themselves!

On the contrary, they seem to have delivered their country to bankruptcy as a result of theft of their country wealth which the politicians shared in one of the biggest robbery in history, and here I call the Sheikh to offer his spiritual advice to those who are ruling over his country, and guide them to such values that for it Imam (Husain) arose, as he believes!

And for the Sunni Sheikh I say to him, in fact I beg him, to deliver a lecture to those young people who are called and tempted by his colleagues Sheikhs through the illusive temptation of the women who are waiting for them in their state battles and campaigns, and those nymphs who are waiting for them in the other imaginary world, when soon after they kill themselves and take the lives of hundreds of innocent people with them, in their promised paradise, and I repeat my question to him: Why he doesn't provide little advise to those who intend and insist to commit suicide in the ugliest way in order to kill the hundreds of innocent victims. Isn't this public hypocrisy enough?

And I don't forget to repeat my advice to the Father, who needs to restore a lecture on ethics to many of the Church followers of those who caused the destruction of the psychological lives of hundreds of children who have been sexually tampered with and abused by those caretakers of the temples of the Lord!"

Here, the Sunni cleric replied with a sharp and upset tone, saying: "Those people you have mentioned do not represent the true religion of Islam which is known for its mercy and compassion to people, and these claims are raised by you who do not believe in the Creator of the universe!"

And the Shiite cleric joined him in favor of a nod of his head and saying that those are nothing but deluded young teenagers who do not know the reality of Islam!

Here, one of the attendance of the general public raises his hand asking for permit to intervene; the host of the meeting welcomed that to ease the sharp debate tension between the participants and speakers, and then the man who seemed to be of a middle age, stood up to talk, and to say:

"I must apologize in advance before I start my comment, because I know it will be hurtful to some of attendees here, but I can't avoid mentioning what I want to say because I don't want to add more redundant words that don't yield benefit, or never lead to the anticipated results, just meaningless redundant words: All what have been said, suggested and portrayed as solutions for such a big problem like this, which I think will be followed by bigger problems if we couldn't reach out to solve it in its beginning.

All of this discussion will practically get us to nothing. I say first to (our Father) if he thought that these people need lessons in the love of (God) for us and our love for (God), and how should this love be, may I ask (our Father) where was the benefit of these lessons when the other (Fathers) who were and probably some of them still sexually tamper with those children who were unfortunate enough to be for a period of their lives under the care of these for a reason or another.

And to the Shiite cleric I ask him: Where were the Shiites in Iraq from the revolution of Imam (Husain), while they have been celebrating and reminded in his principles for centuries, and why don't they revolt against the gangs of clergies and those who live on religion ceremonies, who took advantages of the conditions intended by the political groups in the country who came and claimed power without having any qualification for that, nor deserving to be in the position of leading a rich country, and to eventually transform their country to a very poor collapsing state, begging for help from other countries, after being robed, by both the political and religious parties.

And to the Sunni cleric I ask him: Why doesn't he offer religious exhortation to the people of the Islamic state who enslave women for various reasons and purposes and execute beheading on everyone doesn't approve their behavior and when they don't like his opinion and way of life! And why doesn't he offer the preaching, to those countries that protect such people, and provide them with the financial and media support they need?"

Then, he was interrupted by the three clerics who said that all this is a mixing of the cards, and is not true to say it here. The Sunni cleric went on to add once again that those do not represent Islam, and here, one of the audience stood up suddenly and without asking for a permission from the host of the discussion meeting, to say with an extreme emotional tone:

"Sorry, Sorry, I have something which I feel I must say to everyone and to have it highlighted enough to make it clear to the world! You've stuffed our heads for so many years by these rumors that they do not represent Islam, and perhaps the same thing (our father) would say about those priests and monks that they do not represent Christ (the Lord), and here, I want to say something I have to say it:

I am a Muslim since I was born, and I don't know yet who represents Islam! And I think there are millions like me who think the same as the way I think, and maybe even millions of Christians do the same, but their problem is easier than our problem we Muslims! We Muslims have emigrated from our countries and left everything behind, and today we see those monsters whom you say they do not represent Islam have followed us to the new countries which we were hoping they could keep us away from their dirty living and their brutality!

We fell between the jaws of the pliers! Between those who hate us of people of these communities to which we turned seeking refuge, and those who followed us here to burn all our hopes in a country where we could live in peace. We went through a long period of vetting by the security authorities in order to accept our requests for immigration or asylum, and it was said that it is meant to know our antecedents and previous convictions. We waited for years before we were accepted as immigrants or refugees because of this security check, and today we see thousands of criminals and others who were previously been fighting with terrorists, and others who are believers of radical religious ideologies, all followed us and have been simply and easily admitted and offered the extreme help to assist in and actively play their role in our destruction!

And, all of this going on under slogans we cannot understand their true meanings, such as the slogan of (human rights) which is actually and in reality is meant to keep and serve the criminals, while these slogans show no interest in the rights of the real innocent people who fall in the end under pain and agony and aggression of these criminals. So, what kind of justice those who represent governments of beneficiary politicians are talking and defending? I'm not talking about myself and not only about my new country here, because the same thing is going on in all other countries which are receiving and accepting refugees. Could we say that these countries which accept refugees whoever they are, they want them to be cheap labor? These are the cheap labors who will push your new generations to suicide, because they will not find work which would provide them with the least basics of their needs to live the life they have accustomed to.

At the same time when we see that becoming involved in politics would mostly maintain the privileges and the means to win good income through their political careers even after the termination of their service by the new election or otherwise, our politicians are paid millions of dollars for their talks which they call lectures, lectures of no value, but they represent bribes for the lecturer to pave the ways for the companies to go through all the roads of illegal and disguised ways to ensure their interests not obstructed by law and legislations. This cannot be limited to our country, but it appears in our country in its most horrendous manner, which is in fact the main reason to justify the corruption that is common in other countries of the world, and which are blessed here and protection is provided for these corrupt systems. We the immigrants to this new world, we have had experienced more than enough of suffering when we lived the beginning of our lives when we spent our childhood and youth there in those countries.

And when we have had enough, we decided to emigrate to the new world, hoping to really find the advanced world standards which can provide us with new atmosphere in order to integrate ourselves in this world and give it what we have and at the same time we get its benefits, but we were surprised when we found ourselves equal to those who deliberately came for the purpose to destroy this country, and then the world! We can't accept the view that says these countries of the new world which we thank them for accepting us as new comers to the new homeland, we can't accept that they can't distinguish between those who came in all sincerity in order to integrate in the new world, and those who came with serious intention to destroy civilizations, wherever they could be. Everything is clear even to the naïve and gullible in their thinking, and we started to live in the new type of suffering."

The host of the debate meeting interrupted him by saying: "Do you believe the government did not realize the level of its responsibility towards the people, and what they suffer because of the unemployment rate, which is gradually rising, and without we see the light at the end of the tunnel, at the same time those who are always defending the government say that the problem of unemployment is part of the general problem of the global economy, and I think the time has come to question the (Rabbi) this question in order to know his opinion in this subject."

The Rabbi answered: "It is certainly a problem we all share it, starting from the government to the common people and businesses owners. This problem is a result of the division between the different understandings of how to manage our lives between our capabilities and capacities on the one hand, and our belief in the government to solve the problem!"

"I did not clearly understand the intent of what you meant, Sir, Rabbi, and also, what is more important of this, if you think it is possible to reach a solution to this issue now, and perhaps prevent its occurrence or what is similar to it in the future?"

"There is no problem which has no solution when we want to solve it, and when the will and the desire to solve it is achievable, and this is what I can say in our short, limited meeting!"

"Good, we still have to hope at the end of our meeting that we know more about the developments of this 'call' with the hope that the advocates reconsider it and make it part of the nightmare passing through, and we do not face it another day."

John and a Review with the Soul

John stayed silent, does not want to speak and comment on the latest of what Christine said, until she brought to him his mug of coffee, and asked him again to help her to think calmly and talk about those who brought this (call), which was not in anyone's mind, and it shook their life and raise the whirlwinds and dangerous ideas they did not experience before, and she said to him:

"John, let us seriously think about ourselves and our children, instead of being affiliated to those who can lead us to what we don't know anything about where it would be, nor we know why we give them the right to lead us? I am sure you can think better than whoever wants to think on your behalf, whatever the degree of our relationship with him."

"You know very well I live in a state of frustration for nearly a year, how long you think I can live like this? Can you imagine that?"

"You are not alone living this situation and this frustration, I live it with you, or you don't see that I am so?"

"I know that, but I do not force you to live this life, nor I force you to abandon it, and what I said to you two days ago was only an opinion, which could be a stupid thinking, and you can accept or reject it, I personally can say that I don't expect for myself a better life than this, and I am rejecting this life because it makes me despise myself, and I don't want to live with a permanent contempt for myself, and there will be nothing for me in it, I don't think it is possible to have anything for me in it! Tomorrow will be a day for a gathering when many people who feel like what I feel will be coming to this gathering, some perhaps even have significantly worse feelings towards this life, and I'll see what can be generated in myself after that meeting, and if you like to accompany me to the meeting, which does not require that every one attending would have to be supporting this call, I know there will be many who are media news hunters, as well as many people who enjoy watching the pain of others, you are not one of those, but you are one of those whose ill fortune impose on them to suffer, as a result of their love for others, I know that and I am saying it and I thank you for it, and I very much did not want this to be the end as it is now, with this heaviness and darkness!"

Christine remained silent while listening to his words, she was bowing her head, supported by her hands, looking to the ground, until the telephone rang, so she went to pick up the telephone to see who is calling, her mother was on the line, and she answered her:

"Hello mom, how are the boys doing with you and Dad? I hope they are not causing much trouble to you?"

"No, not at all, your father and I are enjoying their staying with us, they are filling the house of activity, after we as you know have been living with a boring silence."

"Thank God they have not been a big trouble, do you think they are happy in staying with you? I mean especially Tommy; does he miss me that much?"

"Yes, certainly, he remembers you, and wishes if you were here with him, but I tell him you have work for the company you need to do at home, but I must admit he is aware that the school is not in a normal situation."

"Yes, exactly, and I think that this will continue for the next two days, and, mom, I do not feel in a good mood and I'd like to ask you, if possible, if the kids could remain with you the next two days, and I could bring them clothes tomorrow morning, I will be coming with John tomorrow because he also wishes to see them."

"Do not worry Christine I would be delighted to have them for more days, with me and you know it."

"Thank you, Mom and I'll be with you tomorrow morning, I mean, I'll come to visit you and bring them clothes for the next two days, I'll see you tomorrow, Mom."

Christine's telephone conversation with her mother ended, and she felt relatively comfortable, John did not know the cause of it, but he went on asking her: "Why did you ask her to keep the children for two more days? I could have been with them tonight and tomorrow here in the House."

"You are in a position not suitable to withstand children's requests and disturbance, and I will be with you to attend the meeting tomorrow, and it would not be appropriate to ask my mother again to take care of the children tomorrow because I do not want to tell her that we will attend the meeting of this kind!"

"What can you say to your mother if she wondered why the children do not stay with me tomorrow at home and I have no work?"

"I already told her that you are now in the process of checking for more than a chance to work, and I hope that this will be enough, my mother has accepted this excuse, and I don't need to wait for you to change what I have already said to her, we will go tomorrow morning to see the kids and stay with them for half an hour, then make a move together and leave the children with my mother, and let's hope they will not insist that we remain with them for long."

"Let's hope so."

The Street

In the busy streets of the city, the movement was unusual in most facets, the car traffic, the pedestrian people in the streets... but the shops are almost all open, perhaps except some of the stalls selling fast food and some of the simple shops in the open shopping plazas. Between a corner and another, some reporters who are working for few media channels, were carrying microphones and others with the direct live broadcast and recording vehicles and devices, along with cameramen who carry the cameras and follow these live reporters journalists who are searching for whoever they can stop for a few minutes to talk and ask them about what they know about this strange call, and how much they are interested in its news.

As usual, the press became very interested in the news not for its importance, but because it has become an important part of the lucrative work done by the journalists who are rewarded by their channels when they achieve what is called by their terminology a (Unprecedented Journalist Report) when it goes along with the orientation of the media channel for which they work, although in many cases they get nothing from their efforts and reasoning but deprecation of the directors of the channel, and criticize their behavior and consider it not in alignment with the direction of the channel's policy, but in the wrong direction, and therefore, the eventual fate of the journalist in most of these cases is dismissal, without any prior warning!

Some of the bad journalists experiences have been witnesses to the misery of their life, those journalists who put themselves in such predicaments as a result of not heed, and their eagerness to bold venturous action, and the lack of accuracy and truth of the news, they are most often driven by the excitement which can be caused by the way they draft the news, or in many other cases when the news elements often altered!

It is not known which laws govern these journalists service, many of the celebrity journalists fell victims as a result of their extended daring attitudes and their personal reasoning, leaving them in the shooting and criticism spectrum of the State Institutions or the people in general, and the results were the fall of the press into the trap that reinstalled by the events for those who are not careful enough and heed, and then falls into the trap... the ruthless trap!

The press and the media are the two provocative of the events and actions, in a way humanity did not see, before it went through the last quarter of the twentieth century! The whole world has become captivated by the media with all its bad intentions which are mostly devoid of any good intention! Due to this, the proverb suggesting that the press is actually the fourth authority, has been created by the media people who are controlling journalism and the other unseen forces affiliated with it! And if the world could pass the first half of the twenty-first century, the press would very likely become the second authority after the executive authority, when there would no longer be justification and feasibility to have the legislature and the judiciary authorities! Nothing in this world is hard to believe it could happen! In fact, there is no longer anything unbelievable!

At the intersection of two main streets in the busy city center, near the traffic light and the lines of the pedestrian crossings, a reporter of one of the news channels, is electing people from those among passers in front of him, he stops and talk to them, holding a transmitting microphone, and it seems most of those he is stopping them, were not willing to speak on this issue and other subjects that they do not know exactly what they could say about them. Like this issue which the people now are talking about, it is still an introduction waiting to announce for an event or more which could happen, or it could simply end up as rumors! Such a situation is certainly inviting anyone who is always ready to volunteer even when not asked, but doesn't know what his suggestions would yield? This is mostly not common among people who have a lot of concerns and, have no time to please those reporters and satisfy their hunger, for what they could classify as a general and prevailing opinion of the street, according to what their media channels desire, and is coveted by those who sponsor or own the channel!

Actually, what could demonstrate and proves the shallowness of much of what these media channels do in their street random interviews, is what happened when a woman, who must be in her mid or perhaps beginning of the seventies of age, when the reporter walked beside her and very close to asked her: "Madam, can I talk to you for a minute?"

He surprised the woman when suddenly he came too close to her face and almost blocked her way, after she was walking vigorously as much as she had of ability and strength, when she was bending her head towards the ground, and suddenly stopped as she tried to overcome his surprise to her, and after she controlled her walk and managed to hold herself, and realized that he is a reporter when she saw the microphone in his hand and an accompanying cameraman carrying the camera on his shoulder and directing the lens to her direction, she replied with a compliment smile, saying: "Yes, yeah," and fell silent while awaiting what he has to say to her.

"Can I ask you what you know about those people, who everybody is talking about them in the news everywhere, those who intend to commit suicide collectively?"

"Aaaaa, I do not think I have a piece of information that deserves to be mentioned, I am sorry to say this, I heard about this thing, but I did not believe it, is it real?"

"Yes, it is certainly true, but do you think they intend to commit suicide because they belong to a particular religious group, or they have a stand against the government's policy? What do you expect from the reason for their attitude and intention of this?"

"Aaaaa, I don't know, I really don't know anything worthy to say!"

Thus, the reporter tried to pull out of the old woman an attitude or opinion which would go in line with what he wishes for his media channel approval, but it was the sincerity of the people and because they mostly avoid speaking something they do not know, all these were what made this woman say the truth, and the reporter did not like what she said, and if his interview with her wasn't on air, the result would have mostly be deleting this part and keep showing interviews with people whose answers come compatible with what the channel orientations approves. Yes, sometimes they may leave room for another simple statements which they do not approve, so as not to be obvious the manipulation of the interviews.

Just few steps from the site of this reporter and the group working with him, there was another news reporter who works for another channel which is sponsored by an opposite orientation, one of the pro-ruling party channels, and its correspondent, one way or another is doing the same way the first reporter was doing, but he was looking for those who would talk about this in favor of government guidelines, or, at the very least what is taking away the suspicion that the government has a role in creating this situation, in which they called for reflection and collective suicidal as a result of the poor economic situation, which was caused by a method or curriculum economic government and its inability to solve the things that should have been given priority and greater importance, rather than other things which are not related to the people, and do not affect their lives positively. Thus, all the successive governments have considered the society and the people as their experimental fields, and nothing could help the public and save them from the bad results of those experiments, except the good luck of the people when the government intends to apply new laws or programs which sabotage the economy and the development of the country!

This is how, the media continues to take advantage of emergencies, such as this situation in order to come out by itself from the stalemate case which affect it, when there is no exciting and interesting events that could be of concerns and fear among the people, and therefore, the media in fact, in other words, is happy when such tragedies happen, and grieves when they don't happen. This is why we see the reporters always ready to volunteer to go to such tragedies and catastrophic events, travel and incurring difficulties and risks, and it is how journalism became a rewarding career for many of the reporters who make their living on the tragedies of the world, and the media channels subsist on their activities! In many cases, it is no longer possible except for the one who has a high sense and gumption and scrutiny as he deems to discover the media bias, and its factionalism to trench with certain forces associated with certain trends, and the media is nothing more than a profession depends on deception and forgery to gain an audience of people and perhaps push them to their doom!

The reporter took the chance when a young man who seems in his thirties, and his appearance of seriousness and attention through his outfit, as he is wearing a suit which shows he is mostly an employee in an office or a company, and he is carrying a briefcase. The reporter went on towards him carrying the microphone in his hand, in order to show that he wants to talk to him for a quick interview on air, or, perhaps registered, and he greeted the young man by saying: "Hello, can I talk to you for a minute!"

"Aaaa,,,, yes, that is OK!"

"Do you have any idea of what is happening around us lately?"

"Aaaa, I do not understand what you mean by what is happening around us?"

"I mean, you must have heard about this group of people, who intend to commit suicide collectively as objection to many things!"

"Aaaa, yes, what about them, you must know about them more than I know, you certainly are from a news organization and all the news come to you!"

"Yes, we know something but still, the people have their important information, because they are living the reality and are expected to know some of the people involved in this protest, and others who are against what they are protesting! This is why we are trying to convey what some people know to the total or the general public who would mostly need to know!"

"Yes, I can understand this, but my information or the information of the others might be confused, not correct and not true, and therefore, will not contribute to the knowledge of reality of the issue, I could be wrong, as I am sure you know the best way to deliver information to the public, the information which I hope would have a good deal of truth."

"We, as you may know, we also aim at the truth, always."

"This is what I hope!"

"Yes, definitely, but may I ask what type of business you're doing, and forgive me for asking this question, because the feedback seems to me of great value and importance, as what it seems to me, you must be an Executive Officer, maybe an official in a company or,,,"

"No, I am not, actually I am teaching, economics in the university, and my talk with you stems from the importance of the facts, and the need to be ascertained, before we teach them as information and science on the basis of facts!"

"Ah, I can see now the basis of the ability to details the matters, and if I tried once again to ask what do you know about those who intend to commit suicide, could I hear anything maybe you would like the people to know?"

"Actually, I am not well updated with the news, due to my preoccupation with many issues which are related to my work, and I have a belief which might be wrong, that the media chooses some of the issues and events to highlight them, while there may be more important events going on and happening in other locations, I don't know, I might be wrong in this."

"The media does not create events, but only seeks to highlight them, and,,,,"

"Yes, I know that, but you clearly see how it is when a certain event happens at a site and the media hurry up to cover it, the talk and focus become as a whole focused on that event, as if the world on the other sites have stopped moving, or perhaps died, a temporary death, and you know what I mean, so that it is possible to imagine that we are dealing with the news of the trivial events, the worthless, when such big serious events do not happen. In so many cases, I noticed that the media start rumination of ancient events, and trying to repeatedly read them again and again, to portray them for the average people, on the grounds that we should have taken sermon of them, while human history proves the opposite to us when we see mankind did not take a lesson of what people went through of tragic events, which were always liable of passing by in other times, wars have been repeated, and tragedies are always repeated…."

"Thank you again for your time, which you gave us, and we wish you to be away from the bad news."

The reporter withdraw after greeting his last teaching transit guest, after couldn't find enough material and words to satisfy his desire, to rally more support of whatever could assist his opinion,, and what he wants to achieve, with respect to this event, which he seeks to cover, and then he had nothing but to head towards another person, and very likely he does not know yet, how he would talk to him this time?

Bob
Between Past and Present

Bob could not withstand much to resist surrender to his suspicions and presentiment, which are now orbiting the "call", and how it raised the gloom and unpleasant memories of the past, his own past, and what had passed of the days, and how was his intellectual orientation, and something out of these important things insists upon him waiting for a frank answer from him, a frank answer from his inside, a question he does not know why it insists on following him, and is waiting to be answered:

"Would he support the call if it appeared more than forty years ago? If it has appeared at the time when he lived the suffering years with a lot of, if not all, the details of his life? One would wonder if now he has the right to direct his criticism to those who 'call' the others to support them in their 'call' for suicide!"

Bob took himself aside to sit on a chair in the corner of the family room, having finished eating dinner, and the rest of the family stayed on the dinner table: his wife Nicola, his son Jonathan and his wife, and his daughter Josephine. They stayed all sharing different conversations, but he went back to review in his mind all that passed by him today of the time and discussion with Christine, and what accompanied it of perceptions and concerns and memories. How could a man free himself of his unconscious and subconscious mind, or what could be called: The feelings which abstracted off the soul? The feeling which overwhelms humans, including everything outside his soul and his ego!

Bob suddenly noticed when his son Jonathan brought him the mug of tea, and asked him if he doesn't mind sitting with him, and get through his privacy, which was clear and observed by everyone. It was Nicola who indicated it when he split from them, and she also explained to them how his mind has been stormed by this invitation, which he believes its results will not be easy for everyone, and that she shares with him this concerns!

Jonathan sat on the chair opposite his father, and after a few moments of silence, Bob blurted his son wondering, while clearly doesn't seem to care or focus on the importance of hearing any answer: "What will be the second step of your work project?"

"…none, to this moment, we must wait so that we can properly decide if we need to change or add a new technique for the program, the truth is I do not know, the world today is responsive to developments in contravention of many of the logic of expectations, the logic of expectations…"

"Yes, logic of expectations, this is what the new world cannot deal with, not even accept it…"

"Clearly, Dad, you're thinking so much in the cause of this invitation to suicide, do you think it actually could happen? And if it did happen, do you really think it will be widespread?"

"…I will have the answer to your question, by tomorrow!"

"…And what would tomorrow change in the matter?"

"…I will have the ability to see more clearly! Yes, tomorrow I'll have a better ability to answer myself and to answer you!"

Christine
The Battle of the Last Hope

In the morning of the day scheduled to have the meeting of suicides, with other people expected to attend the assembly, to get to know what is this "call", with the expected large number of journalists who seek to do the media coverage, in addition to the people who will definitely attend this meeting out of curiosity, and their desire to watch and know what is an unusual thing, this morning Christine woke up lively, mixed with hope within herself, encouraging her to think that she will succeed in distance the specter of suicidal ideation from her husband John and end this nightmare forever.

She woke up and John himself was awake before her, and he has come down to the ground floor of the house, and sat in the living room with the coffee mug in his hand, which he used to take before breakfast, if he takes breakfast, he has become accustomed since he was working, when he used to leave home early in the morning to pass on his way to the coffee shop close to his home, on the main street, when he used to take a cup of coffee and a piece of (donuts), it was a tradition being carried out by thousands of others who are working away from their home regions, and they need only be present in the workplace early in the morning, where they take coffee with a piece of donuts or cake to be their breakfast, which some of them eat while they are travelling in the car, when it is a long way to work, and in the morning traffic jam.

Christine came down to the ground floor and threw on John the morning greeting, and he returned the same to her, his status was not showing any clear prediction for something in his mind, however, he does not seem to have tendency to talk about anything, but he asked Christine when would they leave towards the house of her parents, she replied that she would be ready within an hour to leave home, he returned to ask her: "What about your going to the office, I mean going to work?"

"... It is not much important to go to the office today, or, at least is not important to go on time, and I'll call the office to leave a message that I will not be in the office in the morning, and after that if I needed to be late, or not to go, I could contact the manager, I mean Bob when I expect him to be in the office, to tell him of being unable to attend today. Oh my God, how I wish things go back to what they were before these days, I wish this day to be a decisive day, so that our life back to normal."

She said that, and meant that John heard what she said, but he remained silent, and did not respond in a comment, any comment. At the hour of leaving home to the house of her parents, Christine took the driving seat in the car, and John sat in the front seat on her side, and he seemed frustrated and psychological signs of weakness, in fact, a total collapse of his inside, he felt as if he is stepping forward toward the fate that no one would like to have, inside himself he feels perhaps he may have hastened his statement to his wife that he intends to participate with those who post those intention on suicide, and since he is truthful with himself, he feels, in a moral obligation to implement what he has announced that he is convinced himself and called his wife to share it with their two children, he only now felt that he has gone fast and unwise in his statement and his enthusiasm to support this call, which is actually true what Christine last night said that she doesn't know what is this "call" when she asked him, do you know who are those who are calling for this invitation.

He is now living a state of lack of self-respect, not only because he is unemployed, but because he may not be able to implement what he said he believed in and is convinced to implement, and now he is trying to find a way out for himself, but he still looks at his life as futile, he is now a burden on his wife, and does not know for how long can this situation continue, now his wife is holding him and strongly sticking to him, but who could guarantee how she would be after another period of time, a period he spends without a job, which is likely a result of what he knows, of what is going on around him, of economic conditions.

Is it fair that the man lives such a state of conflict with his own self? What could he do who wants to maintain his self-respect? Is there a real way, man could retain his realistic and truthful self-respect?

Christine remained silent while driving towards her parents' house, obviously, she was not ready to talk on any subject with John during this period, her mind was like a thrall, tied to what she could see today in the assembly, and how would be her position in it, and how will be her remarks towards reinforcing her view and position of these people, just to distance John away from his conviction that, suicide is the only way out for him and his family from the bad situation he lives in. She has been trying to imagine how will be the shape of this gathering, and who are the people who will be the speakers, how reasonable their words could be, and how logical? How could a man talk in order to convince the people that to commit suicide, is a solution to the personal, social, and soul problems? It will not be an easy task. How would the people receive the words of the speakers? Would there be an opportunity to question any of the speakers?

More importantly, very importantly is, where would be John in this gathering? Will he be with the speakers to this collective suicide people, or will his position be with the suicidal? Then, how, where, and when, can the implementation of this call begin? Could it be mere words without one dare to implement it?

There was a lot, a lot of questions that took place and continued to spin in her head until they arrived her parents' house, and then she stopped her car in front of the garage door of the house, she noticed her father's car was not there, and after they both got out of the car and she rang the doorbell, soon her mother opened the door for them and she was surrounded by her grandchildren Suzanne and Tommy, who showed extreme happiness to see their parents, and both of them were racing to talk about what happened between them and their grandparents last night and how they have enjoyed staying with them.

John embraced his daughter and son, as if he is keen to make his embracing them, a strong reason to stand up for what would keep him longer with them, much longer of what seemed to him the last few days when the dark ideas started to haunt him due to his concerns of leaving his wife and two children, after he dies, and with his own choice, they were moments in which he felt as if he was still somewhat controlling his ability to choose, and before that he felt he is able to distinguish between things, all the bad and the good things alike, he felt that not all the bad things must be rejected, also, that not all good things we need to hold onto them and insist on their possession, it is the other difficult equation in this life!

Christine first question to her mother was about her father, where is he? And the answer of her mother was that he liked going out early in the morning with a group of friends on a trip to the nearby river, to observe the migration of the Salmon fish, which migrates swimming against the flow of water current until it reaches its destination where its mating and reproduction take place.

This trip, the very long (suicidal trip) is carried out by this species of fish to its final, end of life destiny, this of course if they managed to reach these locations where they are mating, since a lot of these fish will be taken from the water by different raptors, hunted by birds of prey when they cross through the shallow water areas of the river, and some of them jump out of the water in an attempt to pass over the rock barriers, and to fall after this attempt on a rock or out of the shallow stream of water to keep battling its overwhelming desire to return to the water, back to life, or the rest of what is left of life, return to life, to water, these desperate attempts would mostly fail, to end up in failure, either die for leaving the water, or, due to being picked up by a bird of prey, or one of the raptor species or carnivorous waiting for this opportunity on both sides of the river!

This is another form of (Invitation to Suicide), which is "called" for and sponsored by nature! And certainly, containing what is stranger than the invitation of those who have lost interest in their own life, for not been rewarded by life, and for their strenuous living, there is still a lot in this life which we can't fathom to this day, we only stand in front of it like the position of an astonished inquirer!

Christine's mother approached her to whisper in her ear, saying she is happy that her father finds pleasure in recent years with some of his friends to go out for short trips hiking, fishing and to enjoy nature. Christine herself is aware when her father was going through years of depression, and now he has obviously passed that period, when the blues and unexplainable thoughts were attacking him, those thoughts which could have not be explained without the advice of a psychiatrist. Even her mother went on to tell her that she is happy that this (call for suicide) did not occur thirty or forty years ago, otherwise, her father would have been expected to be one of its ardent!

"Do you really mean what you are saying? Was my father's condition that bad? This increases my confusion and my fear!"

"Why it raises your fear now?" "No… nothing important, I just find it odd what you are saying because I did not expect that my father condition was once so bad!

"It was, and I did not leave room for you to learn how bad it was! "…So, I did well when I brought Suzanne and Tommy to remain with you last night, it was a good thing… I mean, you have enjoyed your time with them, although I know they must have caused you some trouble as well!"

Christine managed tactfully to avoid the subject of similarities between what her mother did, when she did not leave the opportunity for her daughter, Christine to know what the state of her father at the time of her childhood was, and what she herself did just now. Christine did not leave the opportunity for her children to know something of what is going on in the mind of their father. Christine's mother replied:

"Don't say that. We have lost a lot of what we enjoy in our life, we have nothing left, except quite a few things with which we are trying to bridge the great space of boring emptiness, slow, killer!"

Christine looked at her watch for the time to find out how much time was left, it was about eleven o'clock in the morning, and suddenly her phone rang, it was Bob on the line when his name appeared on the phone screen, she realized he is asking why she did not come to the office, she knows she should have talked to him to tell him about why she did not go to the office today, but she also knows that he will not be strict with her for any reason, especially when he knows that she will accompany her husband to the assembly in an attempt to influence his decision and freeing him from the nightmare of suicidal thinking, she answered:

"Good morning, I know I did not behave decently," "This is not what I want to hear from you, but I wanted to be sure that everything is going well with you and John"

She walked away from the living room where John and her mother sat, in order to continue talking with Bob, and she said to him: "I am sorry I did not call you to ask for your permission not to come today because I'll go with John to this gathering, which I mentioned to you yesterday, or, in fact, I don't recall if I actually have mentioned it or not, the meeting which will be between those who (call) to,,,,,, you know what I mean…"

"Yes, yes,,,,,,, I know that, I am, as I told you, I called you to check on you and John, and not for something else, yes, and the other thing is that I am myself, I did not go to the office today, I do not think I'll go for the remainder of the day, I have called the office and learned that you are not there, this is why I called your phone, tell me how things are going on with John, and what do you think you're going to do there in the meeting place?"

"…I do not know much now, but I have to go, it's my personal battle with them, I will not let them take him from me, I have to be next to him, I see him gradually falling apart minutes after the other"

"This is my eldest daughter, I will always be beside you, I also feel it is my battle, maybe I don't yet know the real reason which push me to this feeling, but it is certainly my battle which I have to win it as well!"

"I will do what I can, and I hope I get good result in that…." "Let me know what happens with you, I am waiting for your news development!"

The call ended, and Christine remained silent and standing in her place for a few moments, holding the phone close to her lips, trying to revive and to retain her focus, and to get ready for her next step, she is still surprised by the intensity of interest Bob is showing in this issue, is it just because she is part of the ground of this "call", represented by the involvement of her husband John who believes in this it? No, No, never, Bob was interested in learning news about this "call" even before he knew that John, Christine's husband is one of the people who are convinced in this "call".

What does this mean? What is it for him to care, or to be interested in what the husband of his secretary thinks or behaves? Something full of a lot of strangeness and confusion! She regained her focus and returned to the room where her husband and her mother were talking when she was on the phone with Bob, the kids were busy with their toys and games, she asked John wondering whether the time has come, she meant from that in front of her mother, it is the appointment for him to have a job interview, and John with a hesitated tone in his response, said:

"Aaaa, yes, I think we must move, in order to catch the interview time!"

They managed to evade their children after they promised to take them to the zoo at the weekend! On the way to the gathering place, John was as he was, silent, gloomy and grim, and does not seem to be interested in anything they pass on along with the movement of the car. He was like someone who was taken to the execution chamber, with his personal usual clothes, he was miserably looking. As for Christine, she returned to her thinking of what she could see at this gathering, and what she would do, in addition to what Bob talked to her.

It wasn't in Christine's mind that Bob himself was on his way to the same assembly!

Bob
Between the Past and
Attending the Gathering!

In the car, on his way to the gathering site, in the largest park in the city of the world financial and professional reputation. The tension was obvious on Bob, he was not the person who controls the movements of his hands, he was confused, hesitant, he felt for a moment the air claustrophobic inside the car, he pressed on the air conditioner button, felt relatively comfortable, but soon noticed the air is relatively cooler than he could stand, the month was late October, and he really felt the pinch of the cold air, then he pressed the button to turn off the air conditioner, moments later he felt a desire to open the car windows to breath fresh cold air, but the current was stronger than he bears its flowing! He closed the car windows again. He wished to find a nearby place where he could park his car, so that he could walk towards the gathering place, although the distance was beyond what he used to walk in such busy streets, and the odds of rain fall, the weather was relatively cloudy, and he does not know what the expectations of the weather are today. Finally, he decided to stop his car in the nearest underground parking lot, in order to continue his way to the gathering site walking.

He reached the main street, crowded with people after he left the parking lot, and started walking towards the park. This is his city which he knows very well, where he began his struggle journey, in fact, his fighting in his major battle. His first fight in his life, which he wishes to be the last and only fight! The only battle against many, many of those who were fighting for the same purpose, for which he was fighting. The attainment of a high degree to which almost every man seeks to reach, or, in more correct words, some of the men, not all of them, perhaps everyone who is ready to crush the others, who posses readiness to bypass the rights of the others, who has the readiness for counterfeiting, fraud and forgery. Readiness for every bad thing that can help achieve the desired purpose, isn't survival only for the fittest? How can he be the fittest, without being able to express all the power and capacity to win in the end.

Don't they say that war is a trick? Could there be honor standards in the wars?! Could there be knighthood and chivalry? Or is this only nonsense talk, and has no truth in reality?

He kept walking bowing his head looking to the ground, trying to avoid looking in people's faces, as if the people who are walking in the opposite direction to him know about what goes on in his mind of memories, open memories which are not limited to specific events, but could this be true and real? Could it be Bob has exceeded the rights of others, blocked them, oppressed them, or denied them? Could it be Bob has ruthlessly crushed other competitors to him in his work? Could it be Bob had caused the suicide of people who had served, and helped him to reach his degree, this degree? What could he do to erase the memory of an unforgettable past?

Suicide Gathering

Christine and John have nearly reached the site or the park area, it was after they were obliged to park their car in a relatively distant side street, and take the streets leading to the public park, where the gathering will take place, and it was remarkable to them that there are a lot of people involved with them in the march in the same direction, obviously for the same destination. The alarm siren sounds of police cars heard from time to time, to confirm that it is unusual and that the police presence, is more than usual in the direction to the park.

Christine, however, grabbed John's hand and both of them walked sometimes vigorously, and at other times lumbering, she wanted to keep her hand with his hand on the pretext of necessity to overcome congestion, when they need to penetrate groups of people, who walk lumbering on the walkway, but obviously she needed at these moments to feel more safe when she is closer to him. In fact, both of them felt inside themselves the need to lift their spirits by being accompanied by each other. This feeling, which is always needed by mankind, despite what goes through the inside of this man during his days of high or low morale!

The tall trees surrounding the big park began to appear from a distance, through the narrow horizon sections appeared in between the short distances separating the high buildings. The crowds and the large number of people increase, as they make their progress towards the gathering center, where it is expected will be something like a podium used by those who intend to talk to people about this "call". The voice of whoever wants to speak to the public must speak loudly to be heard. There has to be a way of loudspeakers, for people who need to hear the reason for this "call". There has to be a talk about announced clear reasons, even if there were hidden reasons.

The talk can't be totally mysterious; there must be clear talk in this mysterious gathering. Mysterious in everything in it!

They arrived at the outer skirt of the gathered crowd. They still can't see who are participating in the "call", and believe in it, from who are only spectators, who record observations inside themselves by looking to their surroundings, wondering where are those who will commit suicide, and where are the spectators? It is only the journalists are clear who they are. They carry with them their declared identities, cameras and microphones for the direct broadcast and for the documentaries. They are the dancers at every ceremony, at every funeral, every joy and every tragedy. One would wonder if this media, including what it owned of capabilities and processing, did or have been actively involved in any remedial conduct action in respect of any of the public serious affairs, maybe, but it is difficult to remember anyone now!

Bob reached the other side of the crowd of people, after his steps began to slow down as he was coming closer to the crowd, all the people looked right heading towards the centre of the pool, waiting for the emergence of a speaker who would be talking to this crowd. Bob was not less motivated than those who are huddled and waiting, eagerly to see who could be a spokesman? And what could he be talking about? What would motivate the speaker and those who affiliate with him, in choosing and supporting this "call", to choose suicide as a solution to their problems? Maybe Bob was even more motivated than many attendees, something makes him interested so much, and with lots of attention to this "call", Suicide!

Between the masses of the crowd, a group of men appeared to gather themselves near the podium, it was what looked like a gathering of football players, to plan before they play, and then one of them split and headed towards the simple podium, which was nothing but a collection of small tables, arranged together in line and supporting each other, and then he ascended the podium, then one of those who were with him in the group came and handed him a loudspeaker, he picked up the loudspeaker, then he started going on walking in a small circle, with short and slow steps to cover his view of the gathering people as he could, those present at this gathering around him, then after a minute or so he raised the loudspeaker close to his mouth, to scream in a strong loud voice, saying:

"Oh life, goodbye, goodbye,
An un regrettable farewell, Goodbye,
It was an unfortunate event! We did not choose, in fact, we could not
choose! We did not have the right to choose! We have not been asked one
day,
What is our choice? We were forced to be part of those who make up this
configuration,
We were told by those who have lived it and finished their journey before
us to call it by the name (Life)!
We don't know who gave it this name!?
That could be one who drew the shape of it, the shape of, this life,
Is he an old King, as old as history?
Or, is he an Emperor who imposed his beliefs on those who submit to
him?
Or, perhaps he is God,
The God we don't know his shape!?
We don't know the truth of his desires and intentions!
We don't know if he would have preferred some of his creatures and
trivialized the others?
We don't know if we have been found in this life to fill in the blanks?
What could be more than the blanks in this miserable unjust life,
Yes, it is so miserable and unjust,
It gathered the extremes,
This might surprise many who hear me, how it is possible for one thing
to be at the same time (miserable and unjust)!
Something difficult to achieve, difficult to happen!
But life did achieve it, it managed to achieve that with us,

At these moments, in the midst of interacting emotions with the powerful words launched by the speaker, those words which were like fireworks, lit the surroundings and corners of a gloomy day, and also brought the clouds to a lower level to cover most of the sky.

John was emotionally shivering as he is trying to combine between focusing on the power of the words of the speaker, and the overwhelming feelings which cause him dispersion between these words which he likes, and what seemed to him that he had seen like it before!! Something like this, when he was sitting alone at home, looking for a job on the Internet, when he was from time to time browsing pages of the YouTube to watch documentaries, where he tends to view history events like the (Bolshevik Revolution) when "Lenin" and his comrades, "Stalin" and "Trotsky" and others, were standing behind him, standing up on platform similar to this, it was "Lenin" who speaks to the people without a loudspeaker, talking about the suffering and struggle of the working class and the capitalist exploitations, and everyone who was watching this scene expressed his admiration for the ability of the man who created the Superpower, after a few years of his ascending that podium, after he lead his revolution to a success!

But how did the revolution succeed? And who was really behind its success? Would it have succeeded without the sacrifices of thousands in the beginning, beginning of the formation of the new state? Was that revolution alone to lead to making a superpower? Without that "Stalin" later, decided to (end the lives) of millions, millions of those whose bad luck brought them in the face of his violence, tyranny, and ruthless, and his continued doubt in all of those who were close to him?

Here, the speaker swaying while talking, using what appears to be a well experienced body language, to achieve greater impact on the audience, or, perhaps on some of them. John, then returned to a wider vision, this vision emerged to him through the words of the speaker on the podium, the tone and glimpses of the speeches of "Hitler", and possibly "Mussolini", when they were preparing to wage the war, the World War II, because of which the lives of millions of people were lost. Those millions of humans were not objecting to the life they were living, and probably were not supporters, or, opposed to those hardened leaders, the savvy in fueling support for their attitudes and beliefs. Wars which they have for long considered as fights and struggles against the hidden forces, and other unopened powers. One would wonder whether this speaker is a suicidal, or his role is to push others to believe and have faith, and then commit suicide?

How many are those of the same kind of this speaker living among us, and in the corners of this world? One would wonder how many like him find listening ears, of heeders who interact and sympathize with what they call? I am wondering if it was right for me to be convinced in this "call", and to have faith in the feasibility of executing it? Or, was it I have been driven out by this injustice in which we live, indefinitely? But, wasn't everything he said true!? Is there anyone who can argue with him!? I don't think it is possible that one would argue with him, anyone in a really convincing argument, otherwise such claims would not have been renewed from time to time? Don't the war calls have compelling reasons!? Wasn't "Lenin" right in most of what he was saying? Wasn't Hitler's complaints, of the bad state of his people a truthful fact, and were witnessed by the world, but shunned it and did not care to what could it lead to!?

Who is the one who separates the disputants in this world!? Is it the right?! What kind of rights!? The right which is often imposed on the defeated! Or the right of the defeated, by not to have the innocent people crushed, the innocent people who did not have hands nor have power in supporting the aggressor, victorious?

During these emotional interactions that were felt by John and left their expressions on his face, Christine was watching him, while holding his hand, she felt in him strongly holding her hand, as if he was actually holding life, and maintaining his commitment to it, those were the heartbeats of life, brought back to him hope and desire, and not to be fuel to the aspirations of others! At the time when he refuses the influence of others on the world, when he is trying to punish them by abandoning and sacrificing himself, his life and his wife and children.

For her, the intensity of his grip on her hand meant a lot of hope to her, which made it clear that she would displace this nightmare she had experienced over the past few days.

John bowed his head, looking down in the middle of the crowd, while the speaker was still going on in his narrative, and increasingly he seemed to be getting more powerful and more influential on people.

Some of the people in the crowd were not known whether they were among those who actually intended to commit suicide, or whether they were media soldiers of that "call," who were putting up their response and their interaction warmly with the speaker, where there were a lot of emotions with heat.

This media, which insists on existing everywhere, seems to have actually managed to pull the rug from under the feet of the human march. News and media, the true and the fabricated, both became the rulers of the fields, all the fields, rulers of what happened yesterday, what is happening today, and what will happen tomorrow and the days after tomorrow.

It has become imperative for people to live with what the media publicize and circulate.

At the other end of the gathering, Bob was standing, listening to every word said by the speaker, listening to him with serious and tense expressions covering his face, blending with them a question and a contraction of brows, showing that he was waiting for what could end the speaker's speech. Nothing was new in what he heard from this speaker's words, the speech. Nothing new to his ears.

It was only that now he heard the words from someone he didn't know, a person whose name he didn't know.

A person whose purpose he didn't know and what he meant by it.

A person whose words he didn't know to what extent they would reach minds.

A person he didn't know how much effect he would have on people.

Someone he hoped to know more than he had heard from him in this position.

But, but is there a need to know all that?

Bob knows himself very well. He knows how he was forty years ago.

Christine remained holding John's hand. She lifted her head to look at him after she had been attached to hearing the speech of this speaker on the podium. Although she didn't interact with it positively or negatively, she lifted her head so her eyes met his. He seemed as if he had just woken up from a deep sleep, just as if he was away from his surroundings, from his mind and all thoughts. Tears were clearly brightening her eyes after she felt they had come too close to the end line.

She was on the verge of collapse.

She felt a desire to embrace him,

begging him to save her from this nightmare, from this darkness that overshadowed all her world. No longer did she feel that she would be able to do more than she had already done.

It had slipped away from her hands. She had no more control over it.

Until John's words knocked on her ears in a wondering tone, asking her, "When can we take the children to the zoo?"